Mini-Fryer Cookery

by Barbara Methven

©1976, 1977 by Publication Arts, Inc., 500 Southgate Office Plaza, Minneapolis, MN 55437. All rights reserved. Printed in U.S.A.
Distributed by Crown Publishers, Inc., New York

Introduction

(Continued from front flap)

showing what they look like, what they're made of, their oil capacity, frying surface and depth, and accessories.

Here are scrumptious meats and main dishes, vegetables, breads, garnishes, and desserts for simple family meals, special occasions, even party fare. Some of the many foods you can make with MINI-FRYER COOKERY are crunchy tostada chips with spicy filling, melt-in-the-mouth Parmesan cheese puffs, a tasty and economical meatball foundue, Chicken Kiev fit for the most demanding gourmet, and exotic Chilies Rellenos. There are also timbale chicken salad delicately spiced with curry powder, tangy orange doughnut drops, a succulent Hawaiian chicken dish, and much more.

A cookbook that will surely revolutionize the American cook's attitude toward frying, MINI-FRYER COOKERY will provide an entree into a new and exciting method for preparing superb food quickly and reasonably.

The mini-fryer makes deep-fried foods an easy and economical way to vary and enliven the home menu. It is especially popular with singles and couples for whom the standard fryer is far too large. Even larger families enjoy the mini-fryer, since it takes only two cups of oil or shortening, stores the oil when not in use, and makes it easy to serve a fried treat with any meal. For most people, cooking with a large standard fryer is a major project which is attempted only occasionally.

Mini-fryers cook one, two or three cups of food at a time, depending upon the type of food cooked, and size of fryer used. If you want to cook additional servings, you can keep the first batch hot in the oven while you prepare the second. Simply preheat your oven to its lowest setting and line a baking dish or jelly roll pan with paper towels. As each batch is cooked, transfer it to the pan to keep warm in the oven.

Many of the recipes in this book are for procedures rather than quantities. They tell you how to prepare dishes and leave the amounts to your own needs. Where quantities are specified, the recipes can be doubled easily.

If your family is large, it would not be practical to cook fried chicken in the mini-fryer, but you'll find it useful for hot appetizers, side dishes, garnishes, fondues and cook-it-yourself parties.

Contents

Introduction 2

Basics of Deep-Fat Frying and Calories 5

Shortening and Oils for Deep-Frying 8

Coatings and Batters 10

Finishing Touches 14

Appetizers 17

Meats and Main Dishes 29

Vegetables 53

Breads and Doughnuts 63

Desserts 69

Slow Simmering .79

Consumer Guide .84

Index 92

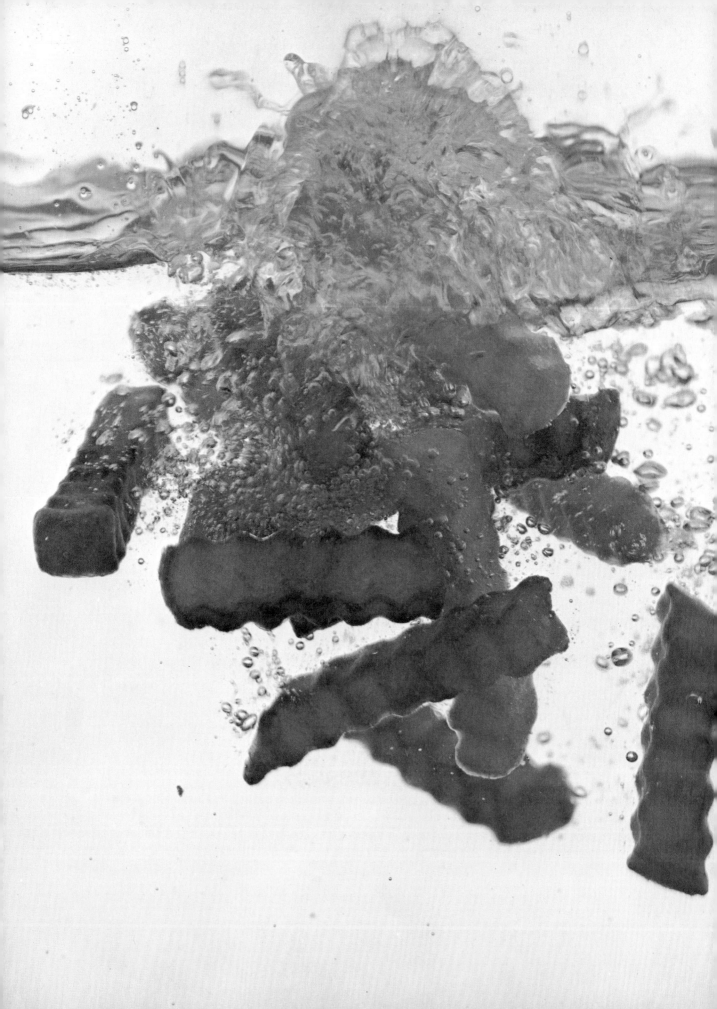

Basics of Deep-Fat Frying and Calories

Many people assume that deep-fried foods are high in calories. While this is true in some cases, it is not true in all. The difference in calorie count between deep-frying and other methods of cooking depends on a particular food's tendency to absorb fat. Some vegetables absorb very little fat and deep-frying them may result in fewer calories than boiling them and dressing them with butter.

Proper frying temperature and short cooking time also reduce fat absorption. The oil or fat should be hot enough to seal the surface of the food quickly and produce a crisp, golden brown crust and tender, delicate interior.

If the temperature of the oil or fat is too low, the food will soak up fat before crusting, and will taste soggy and greasy. When the frying temperature is too high, the outside of the food over browns before the inside is cooked.

If your mini-fryer has a temperature control, set it for desired temperature and wait for the light to turn off before adding food to the oil or fat. Many mini-fryers do not have thermostatic controls, but the preheating time recommended by the manufacturer should bring the temperature to about 375°, which is correct for most foods.

Do not heat the fat until it smokes. When heated to smoking temperature, fat breaks down and may give food a disagreeable taste. Beyond that point, it may catch fire.

To maintain temperature while frying, start with foods at room temperature. Although the temperature of the fat will drop slightly when food is added, it will still be hot enough to crust the food, and will recover rapidly. The exceptions are commercially frozen onion rings, French fried potatoes, and other foods designed to be fried from the frozen state. Follow package directions when preparing these products.

Don't over-crowd the fryer with too much food. This also lowers the temperature of the oil. A few pieces in a single layer with space between them will fry faster, brown more evenly, and absorb less fat.

Frying time and calorie count are directly related. Properly prepared and fried, many meats, fish, poultry and vegetables have fewer calories when deep-fried than they do when pan-fried or sauteed. The high temperatures required for deep-frying seal and cook foods faster, so they are exposed to fat for a shorter time. Anything you do to reduce frying time reduces calories. Most important of these is to fry foods in small batches at the proper frying temperature.

Small pieces (no more than two or three inches thick) also reduce frying time. Try to keep them uniform in size and shape so that all will finish cooking at the same time.

Large items, or foods which take a long time to cook, should be pre-cooked before frying. For example, chicken parts which have been pre-cooked can be deep-fried long enough to heat them through and give them a crisp, golden crust.

Pre-cooking can also reduce a food's tendency to absorb fat. If you enjoy potatoes, but feel French fries are too fattening, try deep-frying well-dried boiled or canned potatoes. They will absorb a minimum of fat, but the crust will give them enough flavor so you won't need the added calories of butter or sour cream.

The mini-fryer provides an easy way to check the fat absorption (and calorie count) of the foods you fry. After straining or filtering the oil and returning it to the fryer, check the oil level. The amount of fresh oil you need to add is a good indication of how much fat your food has absorbed. Of course, some has been lost in draining. However, some foods absorb so little fat that, even with the amount lost in draining, no new additions may be needed. An example is 1 or 2 servings of zucchini fried in Italian Batter.

Finally, a few words about safety. Mini-fryers are designed to accommodate bubbling and spattering, but you should still dry foods well before frying. Use the accessories which come with the fryer or other long handled implements for lowering foods into fat, turning or retrieving them.

All mini-fryers have short cords to protect you against one of the most serious dangers of deep-frying: overturning a pot of hot fat. Even when using the fryer at a table for fondue or for do-it-yourself appetizers, try to position the table to accomodate the fryer's short cord. If you must use an extension cord, be sure it is of the proper weight, and arrange it so that it will not catch on feet or clothing. Burns from hot oil are both painful and dangerous.

Unless your fryer has a thermostat, never preheat it longer than the manufacturer directs. Mini-fryers recover heat rapidly. If you are frying several batches, the oil should be hot enough for the second batch by the time you have removed and drained the first and are ready to fry the second. Unplug the fryer as soon as you have finished frying, or the oil will continue to heat and may reach smoking or flaming point.

If a fat fire should occur, never try to put it out with water or move the fryer to a safer place! Water and movement will both spread the fire. Instead, drop a *metal* pot lid over the fryer and unplug it to prevent electrical fires. Then put out the fire around the fryer with soda or salt; or cover everything with a water-saturated towel.

Preheat oil in mini-fryer (375°). Slip nuts into hot oil and fry 2 to 3 minutes, until crisp. Drain on paper towels. Serve hot or at room temperature.

Variation:

Sprinkle while hot with seasoned salt for an appetizer.

Parsley

Fried parsley is an easy, lacy and attractive garnish for platters or individual plates of food. It melts in your mouth and is delicious enough to be served as a vegetable.

½ **bunch fresh parsley**
1 **egg yolk**
½ **cup very cold water**
6 **tablespoons flour**
   Pinch baking powder

Wash the parsley and shake vigorously to remove excess moisture. Remove coarse stem ends. Spread the parsley on a paper towel to dry. Preheat oil in mini-fryer (375°).

Beat egg yolk, add cold water and beat in flour and baking powder. Holding the parsley by the stem end, twirl in batter, allowing excess to flow back into the bowl. Fry parsley, a few pieces at a time, in hot oil until golden brown.

Drain briefly on paper towel. Repeat with additional sprigs. Serve as soon as all are cooked.

Onion Rings

Homemade French Fried Onion Rings as a side dish are dealt with at length on page 57, but the frozen variety makes it easy to use onion rings as a garnish for green beans, casseroles, salads, steaks or chops. Follow your mini-fryer manufacturer's directions for quantities and times.

Chinese Fried Noodles

2 servings

Fried noodles stay crisp, and can be made early in the day.

5 ounces noodles
   Salt

Boil noodles as directed on package, but cook *no longer* than 5 minutes. Rinse under hot water; drain thoroughly.

Preheat oil in mini-fryer (350°). Fry noodles, a few at a time, in hot oil until puffy and light golden, about 2 to 3 minutes. Drain on paper towels and sprinkle with salt. Serve with a Chinese meal, chicken or steak.

Variation:

Sprinkle with seasoned salt or Parmesan cheese and serve as a snack or a garnish for salads.

The mini-fryer lets you have crisp, hot appetizers in minutes. Many of them need very little advance preparation or planning. Check your refrigerator, freezer or pantry shelf for new and different things to fry. Packaged batter mixes are convenient for those who want to fry appetizers for one or two persons, because they can be mixed in small quantities. Italian Batter can be prepared in the proportion of 2 tablespoons ice water to 1 tablespoon flour.

Several recipes from the Main Dish section also make good appetizers, especially when made in bite-size portions: Meatball Fondue, page 32, Frank Fondue, page 32, Italian Rice-Cheese Balls, page 48 and Small Fritters, page 45.

1. *Chili Con Queso Dip, page 20*
2. *Crisp-Fried Tortilla Wedges, page 20*
3. *Chinese Egg Rolls, page 23*
4. *French Fried Almonds, page 18*
5. *Cocktail Nuggets, page 26*
6. *Parmesan Cheese Puffs, page 25*

Do-it-yourself Appetizer Party

For parties, do-it-yourself mini-fryer appetizers provide variety and contrast with the more common cold dips and nibbles. Choose small items which cook quickly so each guest can prepare a serving in less than a minute. Some suggestions are: Small Mushroom Caps in Buttermilk Batter, page 56; Fried Nuts, page 14; Fried Cheese, below; Hot Fried Olives and Franks in Beer Batter, below and page 32; French Toastwiches, page 25; Cocktail Nuggets, page 26; or Shrimp Chips, available in Oriental food shops, which puff and crisp instantly when dropped in hot fat.

If you are serving at a table or buffet, make sure the cord of the mini-fryer will not catch on anyone's clothing or feet. You may want to place a dish on the table to hold the spoon, tongs or fondue forks when not in use, and a mat under fryer and dish to protect the table surface from dripping oil as appetizers are removed to serving dishes. Provide a stack of small paper plates and paper napkins.

French Fried Almonds

1 cup

1 cup (about 3 oz.) unblanched almonds
1 teaspoon butter or margarine
Plain, garlic or onion salt

Preheat oil in mini-fryer (350°).

Depending upon size of fryer, place ½ to 1 cup nuts in a fine-meshed fryer basket, sieve or wire skimmer. Lower nuts into oil and fry until light golden, 30 to 60 seconds. Immediately turn into a small bowl and toss with butter and salt.

Hot Fried Olives

Drain large stuffed olives and pat dry with paper towels. They are especially good in Beer Batter, or use Italian Batter, Japanese Tempura Batter, Eggless Batter or a packaged mix.

Preheat oil in mini-fryer (375°). Using tongs or fondue forks, dip olives in batter and fry until golden brown.

Fried Cheese

Cut 1-inch cubes or wedges of cheese: Mozzarella, Swiss, Monterey Jack, Cheddar or Camambert. Dip them in Light Crumb Coating or Seasoned Breading. Let dry.

Preheat oil in mini-fryer (375°). With slotted spoon or fry basket, lower cheese into oil and fry until coating is crisp. Do not prick cheese with a fork.

Do-It-Yourself Appetizer Party

Chicken Wings

At least three hours before cooking, prepare Beer Batter, page 13.

Under cold running water, wash as many chicken wings as you will need. Cut off and discard the tip from each wing. Separate the two remaining sections at the joint and discard any fat. Place wing pieces in a saucepan or skillet. Add a small amount of water. Cover and simmer 10 to 20 minutes, until meat appears white. Remove wings and pat dry with paper towels.

Preheat oil in mini-fryer (375°). Dip wing sections in batter and fry them, a few at a time, until crust is light golden brown. Drain briefly on paper towels. Serve with Zippy Tomato Sauce, page 30, or Sweet-Sour Apricot Dip, page 24, if desired.

Popcorn

Although popcorn is not deep-fried, mini-fryers can be used as poppers. The amount of popcorn used will depend upon the variety of popcorn and the size of the fryer.

2 tablespoons salad oil or vegetable oil
¼ to ½ cup popcorn
Salt

Place oil and 2 or 3 popcorn kernels in mini-fryer. Plug in fryer (if fryer has a thermostat, set it at 375°). When kernels pop, add remaining popcorn. Cover with a metal cover or small metal pan. *Do not use a plastic cover.* When corn finishes popping, pour into a bowl immediately. Salt to taste.

Variation:

Sprinkle popcorn with Parmesan cheese or toss with garlic, herb or other seasoned butters.

19

Crisp-Fried Tortilla Wedges

1 dozen 6-inch tortillas make 96 tortilla chips, about equivalent to a bag of corn chips

These hot, tasty chips are a specialty of many fine Mexican restaurants. Combined with the mini-fryer, they are an entertaining appetizer for a party, even when the group is large. The mini-fryer cooks one serving in less than one minute so guests can "do-it-themselves". Instructions are for one package of frozen corn tortillas, but you may use as many as you need.

1 package (14-oz.) frozen corn tortillas, 6-inch in diameter
Dipping sauces

Allow the stack of frozen tortillas to stand at room temperature until it is partially defrosted, and soft enough to separate. With a sharp knife, cut each tortilla into 8 pie-shaped wedges. Place the wedges in a serving dish and when all are cut, cover with plastic wrap and refrigerate until ready to serve.

To cook, the guest slips a few tortilla wedges into the hot oil, occasionally turning and stirring with the slotted spoon until they are crisp. This takes a minute or less. Chips are ready when the frying sounds begin to subside.

The guest removes the chips to a small paper plate lined with a folded paper napkin, salts them if desired and dips them into the sauces.

Suggested sauces:

You may use as many sauces as you like, but you should have at least two, one mild and one hot, to provide contrast. These may be purchased already prepared, or made at home.

Mild sauces: Guacamole, Re-fried Bean Dip or Sour Cream with Chopped Green Onions, below.

Hot sauces: Bottled or canned Taco Sauces, Green Chili Sauce, Chili Con Queso Dip, below.

Sour Cream-Scallion Dip

1 carton (8-oz.) dairy sour cream
2 to 3 green onions, including part of the green top, finely chopped (⅓ to ½ cup)

In a small serving bowl stir together sour cream and onions.

Chili Con Queso Dip

1 medium onion, finely chopped
2 tablespoons butter or margarine
1 can (8-oz.) stewed tomatoes
2 tablespoons canned, chopped green chilies (½ 4-oz. can)*
Pinch salt
½ cup whipping cream
¼ pound Cheddar or Monterey Jack cheese, shredded or finely diced

In a medium saucepan, saute onion in butter until soft and translucent. Stir in tomatoes, chilies and salt. Simmer over medium-low heat until thick. Stir in cream. (May be prepared in advance to this point.)

Just before serving, heat sauce to a slow simmer, stir in cheese and heat until barely melted. Serve warm, using a candle-warmer, if desired.

*Remaining chilies may be frozen for future use.

Tostada Chips

20 pieces

5 corn tortillas, 6-inch in diameter
Filling (below)

Cut tortillas into quarters. Preheat oil in mini-fryer (375°). Fry chips, 3 to 5 at a time, until light golden brown, 1 to 2 minutes. Drain on paper towels.

Just before serving, spread a scant tablespoonful of filling on each chip, going to within ¼ inch of edges. Place chips on baking sheet and heat in a 350° oven 5 to 10 minutes, or until cheese melts.

Tostada Filling

½ pound ground beef
¼ cup chopped onion
¼ cup chopped green pepper
1 teaspoon hot dried chili pepper, optional
1 teaspoon chili powder
½ cup catsup
1 tablespoon taco sauce
½ cup shredded Cheddar or Monterey Jack cheese

In a small skillet, saute beef, onion and green pepper; drain off fat. Stir in chili pepper, chili powder, catsup and taco sauce. Cover; simmer 5 minutes. Spread on Tostada Chips, sprinkle with shredded cheese and heat.

Nacho Filling

1 cup shredded Cheddar or Monterey Jack cheese
¼ cup finely chopped onion
2 tablespoons dairy sour cream or salad dressing
½ teaspoon chili powder

In a small bowl, combine all ingredients. Spread on Tostada Chips and heat.

Tostada Chips with Nacho Filling and Tostada Filling

21

Savory Fried Turnovers

25 pieces

Turnover Pastry (page 42)* or a mix
½ cup filling

Prepare pastry for a 1-crust pie. Be sure it is moist enough so it will not crack when rolled out or folded. Roll out on floured pastry cloth to a 13-inch square. Trim edges to make a 12½-inch square. Cut into 25 2½-inch squares by making 4 cuts in each direction with a pastry wheel or sharp knife. Place a teaspoonful of filling on half of each square. Moisten edges. Fold over to form rectangles and seal edges with a fork. Turnovers may be made early in the day, covered and refrigerated until 15 minutes before frying time.

Preheat oil in mini-fryer (375°). Fry turnovers, a few at a time, until light golden brown, about 3 minutes, turning to brown both sides, if necessary.

*For extra-crisp turnovers, substitute egg roll skins (6 to 7-inch), cut in quarters. Use 1 tablespoon filling. Brush well with beaten egg before sealing.

Savory Turnover Fillings

Ingredients for turnovers should be finely chopped and well-blended so they can be enclosed in the pastry. Use 1 scant teaspoon filling for each turnover. Select one of the combinations below, or make your own using leftover meat, deli or canned sandwich spread.

Ham or Sausage & Cheese: ⅓ cup finely chopped ham, salami, summer sausage or bologna and 3 tablespoons finely cubed cheese.

Hot Dog: ½ cup finely chopped bologna or wieners. Dot each pastry with catsup.

Beef & Pickle: ½ cup (¼-lb.) lightly fried ground beef, drained, and 2 tablespoons pickled relish or catsup

Chili Beef 'n' Cheese: ⅓ cup lightly fried ground beef, drained, 2 tablespoons catsup, 3 tablespoons finely cubed cheese and ½ teaspoon chili powder.

Tuna Cream Cheese: ⅓ cup tuna or salmon, well drained, ¼ cup (2-oz.) softened cream cheese or dairy sour cream, 2 tablespoons finely cubed Cheddar cheese and ½ teaspoon caraway seed.

Shrimp & Sour Cream: ½ cup chopped, cooked shrimp, 2 tablespoons dairy sour cream and 1 teaspoon dill weed.

Onion-Pepper: ¼ cup (2-oz.) softened cream cheese or dairy sour cream, ¼ cup finely chopped onion, 2 tablespoons finely chopped green pepper, ½ teaspoon caraway seed and a pinch of salt.

Ham & Cream Cheese: ¼ cup (2-oz.) softened cream cheese and ⅓ cup finely chopped ham, salami, summer sausage or bologna.

Wieners in Blankets: Cocktail wieners or wieners cut in half lengthwise and then into thirds crosswise. Dot each with prepared mustard and wrap in pastry.

Egg Rolls

Egg Rolls make popular appetizers and can also be served as a main dish for lunch or supper.

8 egg roll skins (½ pound), 6 to 7-inches square*
1 small egg, beaten
Filling (below & next page)

Prepare and cool filling, if necessary. To wrap egg rolls, lay a skin on work surface with one of the points toward you, forming a diamond. Place ¼ cup filling just above the center of the diamond. Fold top point over filling, then fold side points over top point. Moisten all edges with egg. Starting from the top, roll toward the bottom point, pressing firmly to enclose filling. Make sure all edges are sealed well. Rolls may be shaped in advance and refrigerated, then fried just before serving time. Preheat oil in mini-fryer (375°). Fry 1 to 3 rolls at a time until golden brown, 1 to 2 minutes on each side. Drain on paper towels. Cut in 2 or 3 pieces to serve as an appetizer, leave whole for a main dish or snack. Serve hot with suggested sauces.

*For individual egg rolls, cut skins in quarters. Use 1 tablespoon filling. Roll up and seal, as directed above.

Chinese Egg Roll Filling

fills 8 rolls

1 teaspoon sugar
½ teaspoon salt
1 teaspoon cornstarch
1 tablespoon soy sauce
2 tablespoons salad oil
1 small to medium pork chop, cut in very small dice
½ cup chopped raw shrimp (3 to 4 large fresh or frozen, defrosted)*
½ cup finely chopped celery
¼ cup finely chopped fresh mushrooms
4 small green onions, chopped
4 water chestnuts, chopped
¼ cup finely chopped bamboo shoots or bean sprouts, well drained

Have ingredients ready before starting to cook. In small bowl, combine sugar, salt, cornstarch and soy sauce; set aside. Heat oil in wok or large skillet. Add pork, stir-fry 2 minutes, or until it loses red color. Add shrimp, stir-fry 30 seconds. Add vegetables, stir-fry 1 minute. Remove from heat; toss with soy mixture. Cool. Fill skins. Serve with Hot Mustard and Sweet-Sour Apricot Dips, page 24.

*If tiny or chopped, cooked shrimp are used, add at the end.

23

Pizza Filling

fills 8 rolls

½ pound ground beef
½ cup finely chopped onion
½ cup finely chopped celery
 1 can (2-oz.) mushroom pieces,
   drained and chopped
½ teaspoon sugar
½ teaspoon salt
¼ teaspoon oregano
¼ teaspoon basil
¼ teaspoon parsley
 1 small clove garlic, finely chopped
½ cup tomato sauce
½ cup shredded Mozzarella cheese

In a medium-size skillet, saute beef
and onion; drain off fat. Stir in
remaining ingredients except cheese.
Simmer, uncovered, until thick, about
10 minutes. Cool. When filling egg
rolls, top each with a tablespoon of
cheese before wrapping.

Ham and Cheese Filling

fills 8 rolls

 1 cup chopped ham, bologna,
   wieners or other luncheon meat
 1 cup shredded Cheddar, Swiss or
   Mozzarella cheese
½ cup finely chopped celery
 2 tablespoons finely chopped onion
 1 tablespoon prepared mustard
 1 tablespoon mayonnaise

Combine all ingredients in a small
bowl. Serve with Sour Cream
Horseradish Sauce, page 30.

Variation:

Reuben Rolls: Substitute corned beef
for ham and well-drained chopped
sauerkraut for celery. Makes a good
supper ''sandwich'', too.

Easy Chicken Egg Roll Filling

fills 8 rolls

1¼ cups finely chopped cooked
   chicken, turkey, pork or
   shrimp, or a combination
¾ cup finely chopped celery
¼ cup finely chopped green onion
¼ cup finely chopped water
   chestnuts
¼ cup finely chopped mushrooms,
   fresh or canned (2-oz.)
 2 tablespoons soy sauce
 1 teaspoon sugar
 1 teaspoon monosodium glutamate,
   optional
½ teaspoon salt
½ beaten egg (about 2 tablespoons)
   reserve remainder for sealing
   egg rolls

Combine all ingredients in a small
bowl. Cover and refrigerate at least 1
hour. Drain off all juices before filling
egg rolls. Serve with Hot Mustard Dip
and Sweet-Sour Apricot Dip, below.

Sweet-Sour Apricot Dip

⅔ cup

½ cup apricot preserves
 1 tablespoon chopped pimiento
 2 teaspoons vinegar
 1 tablespoon water

Combine all ingredients in a small
saucepan. Bring to a boil, cook 1
minute, stirring constantly.

Hot Mustard Dip

1 tablespoon dry mustard
  Few drops water

In a small dish, blend together mustard
and water to make a soft paste.

French Toastwiches

16 pieces (4 to 8 servings)

These deep fried sandwiches also make an excellent lunch or supper.

8 slices day-old white bread, trimmed of crusts

4 slices Mozzarella, Monterey Jack or Cheddar cheese, cut ¼-inch thick and about the same size as the bread

2 eggs

¼ cup milk

½ teaspoon salt

1 cup fine, dry, unseasoned bread crumbs, spread on a plate or waxed paper

Place cheese slices on 4 slices of bread. Cover with remaining 4 slices and press lightly so that layers adhere. Cut each sandwich into 4 squares or triangles.

In a baking dish large enough to hold the sandwiches, beat the eggs lightly. Stir in the milk and salt. Dip edges of the sandwich quarters into the egg mixture, then turn them in bread crumbs to coat well. Place sandwich quarters in the dish, turning them to coat both sides. Cover the dish and refrigerate until ready to serve.

Preheat oil in mini-fryer (375°). Using a pancake turner or slotted spoon, slip the sandwich quarters into the hot oil. Fry them a few at a time, until golden brown on both sides. Drain briefly on paper towels and serve hot.

Variation:

Sprinkle the cheese with crisp-fried, crumbled bacon before adding the second slice of bread.

Parmesan Cheese Puffs (Profiteroles)

24 pieces

Profiteroles are easy, melt-in-the-mouth appetizers made from cream puff dough. Try them for a do-it-yourself party.

½ cup hot water

¼ cup butter or margarine

½ cup all-purpose flour

¼ teaspoon salt

2 eggs

¼ cup grated Parmesan Cheese

In a small saucepan, melt butter in water. Bring to a full boil and reduce heat to low setting. Remove pan from heat and stir in flour and salt. Return pan to heat and cook, stirring constantly, until mixture forms a smooth, compact ball, about 2 minutes. Remove from heat. Add eggs, one at a time, beating vigorously after each addition. Continue to beat until dough is smooth and glossy. Stir in cheese and mix well.

Preheat oil in mini-fryer (350°). Drop dough by rounded teaspoonfuls into hot oil. Fry until golden brown, 3 to 5 minutes. Serve hot. May be kept hot in a 250° oven. Extra dough may be covered and stored in the refrigerator a day or two, but the puffs will brown faster.

Variations:

Riviera Cheese Puffs: Add ½ cup diced ham, 2 chopped anchovies (optional) and ¼ cup toasted slivered almonds with the cheese. (Almonds may be deep-fried in a small strainer for 30 seconds.)

Seafood Cheese Puffs: Add ½ cup drained, chopped oysters or ½ cup tiny or chopped, cooked shrimp with cheese.

Cheese-Olive Nuggets

Cocktail Nuggets

These delightful morsels will be the stars at any party.

2 to 2½ dozen

Filling (below)
2 to 3 tablespoons flour
1 egg, slightly beaten with 2
   teaspoons water
½ to 1 cup fine, dry, unseasoned
   bread crumbs

Prepare filling. Shape into 1-inch balls. Roll in flour, dip in egg mixture and turn in bread crumbs to coat well. (When making Bacon-Olive Nuggets and Cheese-Olive Nuggets, repeat the process for a firmer coating.) Preheat oil in mini-fryer (375°). Fry nuggets until golden brown, as directed with the filling recipes. Drain on paper towels. Serve warm with suggested sauces if desired.

Unfried Nuggets may be made in advance and frozen. Frying time for frozen Nuggets will be only 1 to 2 minutes.

Tuna-Olive Filling

1 can (6½-oz.) tuna, well drained
½ cup shredded Cheddar cheese
½ cup finely chopped ripe olives
⅓ cup dairy sour cream
¼ cup fine, dry, unseasoned bread
   crumbs
1 teaspoon caraway seed
½ teaspoon salt

In a small bowl, combine all ingredients thoroughly. Fry finished balls 1 to 2 minutes.

Cheese-Olive Filling

1 cup shredded Cheddar cheese
½ cup chopped stuffed green olives
⅓ cup dairy sour cream
¼ cup fine, dry unseasoned bread
   crumbs
Dash cayenne

In a small mixing bowl, combine all ingredients thoroughly. Fry finished nuggets 1 minute.

Bacon-Olive Filling

¼ to ½ pound bacon
1 package (8-oz.) cream cheese, at
   room temperature
½ cup finely chopped pimiento-
   stuffed green olives
3 drops smoke sauce, optional
½ cup finely chopped celery

Fry bacon until crisp. Crumble into small bowl and let cool. Mix in remaining ingredients thoroughly. Fry finished nuggets 1 minute. No sauces are needed.

Reuben Filling

2 tablespoons finely chopped onion
1 tablespoon butter or margarine
1 tablespoon flour
2 tablespoons milk
½ cup finely chopped corned beef or
   ham*
¼ cup (½ of 4-oz. can) sauerkraut,
   well drained and finely chopped
½ cup shredded Mozzarella or Swiss
   cheese

In a small saucepan, saute onion in butter. Blend in flour; stir in milk. Cook over medium heat, stirring constantly until thick. Refrigerate until chilled. Stir in remaining ingredients thoroughly. Fry finished balls 1 to 2 minutes.

*Corned beef and sauerkraut may be chopped in the blender.

Mexican Beef Filling

1 cup lean uncooked ground beef
2 tablespoons finely chopped onion
2 tablespoons finely chopped green
   pepper
1 celery rib, finely chopped
1 cup shredded Monterey Jack or
   Cheddar cheese
2 tablespoons catsup
2 teaspoons chili powder
½ teaspoon salt
2 twists freshly ground pepper

In a small bowl, mix all ingredients together thoroughly. Fry finished balls 3 minutes. Serve with Zippy Tomato Sauce, page 30, Barbecue Sauce or Guacamole Sauce.

Oriental Shrimp Filling

2 tablespoons butter or margarine
2 tablespoons flour
¼ cup milk
4 water chestnuts, finely chopped
¼ cup finely chopped celery
2 green onions, finely chopped
1 cup tiny or chopped cooked
   shrimp
½ teaspoon monosodium glutamate
1 tablespoon Japanese soy sauce
1 slice ginger root, finely chopped,
   optional

Melt butter in a small skillet. Blend in flour. Stir in milk. Refrigerate until chilled. Stir in remaining ingredients thoroughly. Fry finished balls 1 to 2 minutes. If desired, serve with Hot Mustard Dip, page 30, and Sweet-Sour Apricot Dip, page 24.

Meats and Main Dishes

With a mini-fryer, singles and couples can enjoy fried main dishes without heating the excessive amounts of oil needed for a standard fryer or electric skillet. Most of our recipes are for 2 people and include meat, poultry, fish, cheese and egg dishes.

Many appetizers also make good main dishes for lunch or supper. Try Egg Rolls, page 23, French Toastwiches, page 25, or Mexican Beef, Tuna, Shrimp or Reuben Cocktail Nuggets, page 26, allowing 7 to 8 per serving.

For 2 to 6 people, the mini-fryer makes a perfect pot for fondue and other at-the-table frying. Fondue is popular party fare, but is also an easy way to make an occasion of a family meal. The mini-fryer is safer for use with children than a fondue pot with an alcohol burner, but children should not fry their own food without adult supervision.

Mini-fryers make a fondue party easy. Sauces, top to bottom, are: Sweet-Sour Apricot Dip, page 24, Sour Cream Horseradish Sauce, page 30, Zippy Tomato Sauce, page 30.

29

Fondue Bourguignonne

4 servings

1½ to 2 pounds lean tender, boneless beef, cut in 1-inch cubes
3 to 4 sauces, made at home or purchased from the gourmet section of the supermarket

Suggested Sauces:
  Hollandaise, below
  Curry or Mustard Dip, below
  Sour Cream Horseradish, below
  Zippy Tomato Sauce, below
  Sweet-Sour Apricot Dip, page 24

To serve: Provide each person with a fondue fork for cooking and a table fork for eating. Place a mat under the mini-fryer to protect the table. Preheat oil in mini-fryer (375° - 400°). Each person spears a piece of meat on the fondue fork, dips it in the hot oil, and cooks it to desired doneness.

Serve with crusty French bread and a green salad garnished with avocado slices and fried pecans, page 14, and tossed with oil and vinegar dressing.

Caution: Be sure to unplug the mini-fryer as soon as cooking is completed.

Hollandaise Sauce

⅓ cup

1 egg yolk
1 teaspoon water
1 tablespoon lemon juice
¼ cup firm butter or margarine
  Salt and pepper

In small saucepan, beat together egg yolk, water and lemon juice with rubber spatula until well blended. Add butter; cook over lowest heat. Stir constantly until mixture thickens. Season. Serve hot or cold.

Curry or Mustard Dip

¼ cup (2-oz.) cream cheese, softened
⅓ cup dairy sour cream
1 teaspoon grated onion
¼ to ½ teaspoon curry powder or dry mustard*
  Pinch salt

In a small bowl, blend all ingredients together thoroughly.

*Substitute ½ to 1 teaspoon prepared mustard, if desired.

Sour Cream Horseradish Sauce

1 carton (8-oz.) dairy sour cream
¼ cup horseradish
½ teaspoon Worcestershire sauce

In a small serving bowl, combine all ingredients. If desired, add more horseradish to taste.

Zippy Tomato Sauce

1 cup

1 cup catsup
2 tablespoons water
2 tablespoons finely chopped green onion
2 tablespoons finely chopped green pepper
  Dash tabasco sauce

Combine all ingredients in a small saucepan. Simmer 5 minuts, covered. Serve hot or cold with shrimp, fish, beef or frankfurter fondue.

Variation:

Quick Italian Sauce: Substitute 1 can (8-oz.) tomato sauce for catsup and 2 tablespoons dry wine for water. Add 1 clove pressed garlic and ¼ teaspoon oregano leaves.

Japanese Fondue

4 servings

Both adults and children will eat vegetables with enthusiasm when you serve fondue Japanese style.

1 to 1½ pounds flank steak; or
    cubed, lean, tender beef; or
    4 half chicken breasts, skinned
    and boned
4 or more of the following:
    2 large green peppers, seeded,
      de-ribbed and cut in 1-inch
      squares
    8 scallions, including part of the
      green, cut in 1-inch lengths
    8 large fresh mushrooms, cut in
      halves
   12 tender, fresh green beans
    1 sweet potato, peeled and cut in
      ¼-inch thick slices
    1 can bamboo shoots or water
      chestnuts, rinsed and drained
    4 small green tomatoes, cut in
      quarters
  Teriyaki Sauce (bottled)
  Tempura Sauce (page 37)

If you are using flank steak: trim away any fat and cut the flank steak lengthwise into strips 1½-inches wide, then crosswise into ¼-inch thick slices.

If you are using boned chicken breasts: remove the small tube-shaped fillet and pull out the tendon. Lay the pieces of meat on a sheet of waxed paper and cover with a second sheet. Using the side of a cleaver or the bottom of an iron skillet, pound the breasts lightly to flatten them. Cut the small fillets crosswise into 2 pieces. Slice the larger fillets lengthwise into strips 1-inch wide, then crosswise in pieces 1½ to 2-inches long.

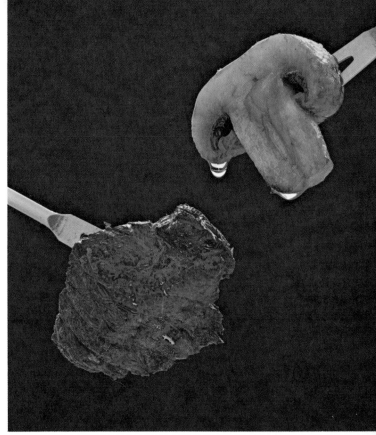

Japanese Fondue

Arrange portions of meat and vegetables on 4 dinner plates; cover with plastic wrap and refrigerate.

Measure the sauces into 8 small bowls or cups. Set them aside at room temperature.

To serve: Provide each person with 2 fondue forks for cooking meat and vegetables, and chop sticks or a table fork for eating. Arrange bowls of dipping sauce at each place. Put a mat under the mini-fryer and preheat the oil (375°). Pat the foods with a paper towel to make sure they are dry.

Each person spears a piece of meat on one fork and a vegetable on the other, then dips them in the hot oil. They will cook very rapidly, and are dipped in a sauce before eating.

Serve with bowls of hot steamed rice.

Caution: Be sure to unplug mini-fryer when cooking is completed.

Meatball Fondue

4 servings

For fondue lovers, meatballs make a delicious and economical alternative to steak.

1 egg, lightly beaten
1 pound lean ground round steak
½ cup very fine, dry bread crumbs
2 tablespoons finely chopped onion
1 teaspoon salt
  Pinch pepper
  Light Crumb Coating (page 11) or
    Beer Batter (page 13), optional
2 to 3 sauces

Suggested Sauces:
  Sour Cream Horseradish, page 30
  Mustard Dip, page 30
  Zippy Tomato Sauce, page 30

In a medium mixing bowl, thoroughly combine eggs, ground round steak, crumbs, onion, salt and pepper. Form mixture into balls, 1-inch in diameter. If desired, bread meatballs with Light Crumb Coating or prepare Beer Batter and divide into 4 individual bowls.

To serve: Follow directions for Fondue Bourguignonne, page 30.

Variations:

Rather than serve meatballs as a fondue you may prepare a double recipe of one of the following sauces in a wide, shallow pan. Fry meatballs, a few at a time, and set them aside on paper towels to drain. When all are cooked, add them to the sauce and warm for a few minutes over very low heat.

Hawaiian Meatballs: Sweet-Sour Sauce, page 38 (with pineapple chunks) with plain or Beer Battered Meatballs.

Roman Meatballs: Quick Italian Sauce, page 30, with plain or Crumb Coated Meatballs.

Meatball Stroganoff: Stroganoff Sauce, page 33, with plain or Crumb Coated Meatballs.

Frank Fondue

4 to 5 servings

Children will love this; so will guests as a do-it-yourself appetizer.

  Beer Batter (page 13)
1 package (12 or 16-oz.) frankfurters
  or wieners
2 or 3 sauces

Suggested Sauces:
  Mustard Dip, page 24
  Zippy Tomato Sauce, page 30
  Sweet-Sour Apricot Dip, page 24
  Apricot Curry Sauce, page 34

Prepare Beer Batter at least 3 hours in advance. Cut frankfurters into 1-inch pieces. Dry very thoroughly with paper towels.

To serve: Follow directions for Fondue Bourguignonne, page 30, providing each person with a small bowl of batter in which to dip franks before frying.

Variation:

Corn Dog Fondue: Substitute packaged corn dog mix for Beer Batter.

Sweet-Sour Deep-Fried Pork or Beef

2 servings

Sweet-Sour Sauce (page 38)
2 servings boneless pork loin or tender beef, raw or cooked
1 egg white
1 tablespoon cornstarch
2 teaspoons soy sauce

In a wide, shallow pan large enough to hold sauce and meat, prepare Sweet-Sour Sauce, adding fruits and vegetables as desired.

Cut meat into strips about 3 inches long; raw meat ⅛-inch thick and cooked meat ¾-inch thick. In a small bowl, blend together egg white, cornstarch and soy sauce. Add meat and toss gently to coat. Preheat oil in mini-fryer (275°). A few pieces at a time, fry meat until golden brown and crisp, about 2 minutes. Drain on paper towels. Reheat sauce, if necessary. Add meat and heat through. Serve over hot steamed rice.

Deep-Fried Beef or Pork Stroganoff

2 servings

Stroganoff Sauce (below)
2 servings boneless, tender beef or pork loin, raw or cooked
For pork, Egg Batter (page 12), optional

In a wide, shallow pan large enough to hold sauce and meat, prepare Stroganoff Sauce, but do not heat sour cream.

Cut meat into strips about 3 inches long; raw meat ⅛-inch thick, cooked meat ¾-inch thick. Flour pork or dip in Egg Batter.

Preheat oil in mini-fryer (375°). A few pieces at a time, fry beef about 1 minute or pork until brown and crisp, about 2 minutes. Drain on paper towels. Add to sauce and heat through, but do not boil. Serve over hot cooked noodles.

Stroganoff Sauce

about 1 cup

½ cup sliced fresh mushrooms, or 1 can (4-oz.) drained*
2 tablespoons chopped onion
2 tablespoons butter or margarine
2 teaspoons flour
1 teaspoon instant beef bouillon granules
¼ teaspoon beef gravy extract
½ cup water
⅓ cup dairy sour cream
Salt
Pepper

In a small skillet, saute mushrooms and onion in butter. Stir in flour, bouillon granules, beef extract and water. Cook, stirring constantly until thickened and smooth. Just before serving, stir in sour cream, salt and pepper; heat through but do not boil. Serve with deep-fried beef, pork, chicken or croquettes.

*If using canned mushrooms, reserve juice and substitute for part of the water.

Deep-Fried Precooked Chicken Fryer Pieces

Separate wings from breast pieces and drumsticks from thighs. Steam or simmer in salted water 15 minutes. If desired, add a slice of onion and celery rib to cooking water. Drain chicken and pat dry.*

Have chicken pieces at room temperature. Coat with flour, shaking off excess. Use Light Crumb Coating for breaded chicken, or dip in Egg, Light and Fluffy, Eggless or Beer Batter, page 11 - 13.

Preheat oil in mini-fryer (365°). Fry 1 or 2 pieces at a time, depending on size of pieces and fryer, until oil stops bubbling and chicken is light golden brown, 12 to 15 minutes.

When frying several servings, you may keep the first pieces warm in an oven preheated to its lowest setting, or re-crisp the coating by returning them to the fryer for a minute or two. Serve with lemon wedges, Apricot Curry Sauce, below, or Barbecue Sauce.

*Small drumsticks and wings may be fried without precooking, if desired. They will take 15 to 18 minutes.

Apricot Curry Sauce
½ cup (scant)

⅓ cup apricot preserves
1 tablespoon butter or margarine
1 teaspoon lemon juice
½ teaspoon curry powder

Combine all ingredients in a small saucepan. Heat, stirring constantly, until butter is melted and sauce is hot.

Deep-Fried Uncooked Chicken

Use boned chicken breasts. Cut in 1-inch cubes, or divide each breast section into two pieces. Marinate if desired, recipe below. Pat dry with paper towels, coat with flour and shake off excess. Dip in Egg Batter, page 12.

Preheat oil in mini-fryer (365°). A few at a time, fry pieces 8 to 10 minutes, or cubes 3 to 5 minutes, until golden brown. Serve as suggested for Precooked Chicken, or reheat briefly in Sweet-Sour Sauce, page 38, or Stroganoff Sauce, page 33.

Marinade for Uncooked Chicken

⅓ to ½ cup

¼ cup Japanese soy sauce
1 tablespoon brown sugar
1 tablespoon lemon juice
1 tablespoon finely chopped onion
  Thin slice fresh ginger root, optional

Combine all ingredients in a small bowl or shallow casserole. Add chicken and turn to coat well. Let stand in refrigerator 30 to 60 minutes, or longer.

Chicken Kiev

2 to 3 servings

3 half chicken breasts, skinned and boned
  Chopped chives or green onion
  Snipped parsley
  Salt
  Pepper
3 sticks cold butter, 2×⅜-inch
2 to 3 tablespoons flour, spread on a plate or waxed paper
1 small egg, beaten
½ cup fine, white and untoasted bread crumbs

Place breast halves, cut side up, on a sheet of plastic wrap. Cover with a second sheet. Flatten with mallet or flat side of cleaver until very thin, ⅛ to ¼-inch thick. Remove top sheet of plastic. Sprinkle meat lightly with seasonings.

Place stick of butter at end of each piece. Fold sides of breasts up to cover ends of butter sticks. Roll up, completely enveloping butter. Press firmly to seal. Fasten with wooden picks, if necessary.

Roll in flour, dip in egg, making sure all surfaces are completely coated. Shake off excess. Roll in crumbs, coating thoroughly. Fry immediately or refrigerate so that butter does not soften.

Preheat oil in mini-fryer (365°). Depending upon size of fryer, fry 1 to 3 at a time until deep golden brown, 7 to 10 minutes. If frying in several batches, keep first pieces warm in oven preheated to lowest setting.

Tempura

2 servings

½ pound raw shrimp, peeled and
    deveined, with tails left on, or ½
    pound fish fillets, cut in slices
    ¼-inch thick
4 or 5 items from list below:*
    6 green pepper strips or rings
    3 mushrooms, cut in half
    6 slices or sticks zucchini
    6 slices or sticks eggplant, salted
      and drained
    6 onion rings or 1½-inch lengths
      scallion
    6 snow peas, fresh or frozen,
      defrosted
    6 fresh green beans, blanched
    6 slices peeled sweet potato,
      ¼-inch thick
    6 sprigs parsley
    6 pieces peeled broccoli
    6 fresh asparagus spears
Japanese Tempura Batter
    (page 12)
Tempura Sauce (below)

When slicing the vegetables, try for contrast in color and shape. If you are using both zucchini and eggplant, cut one in slices and the other in strips. When combining green beans and peppers, cut the peppers in rings or use sweet red peppers.

Arrange seafood and vegetables in an attractive pattern on a platter. Cover with plastic wrap and refrigerate. Prepare Tempura Sauce.

Tempura is usually served as a main course but it can also be served as a delicious appetizer.

Cook Tempura at the table or on a nearby counter. Place a mat under the mini-fryer to catch drips of batter and oil. Place several thicknesses of paper towel on a cake rack over a plate or baking dish to serve as a draining tray. Provide each person with a cup of sauce, a plate or basket lined with a paper napkin or towel, and a fork or chop sticks for eating. Preheat oil in the mini-fryer (375°) while you prepare the batter.

One piece at a time, dip foods into the batter and slip them into the hot oil. Depending upon size and shape, you may fry 3 to 6 items at a time. As soon as they are golden brown on all sides remove them with the slotted spoon and drain briefly on the cake rack. Diners transfer the foods to their baskets and dip them in the sauce as they eat.

Serve with hot steamed rice.

Caution: Be sure to unplug mini-fryer when cooking is completed.

*Special instructions for each vegetable are given in the vegetable section.

Tempura Sauce

1 serving

1 tablespoon sugar
2 tablespoons chicken broth
1 tablespoon Japanese soy sauce
1 teaspoon sweet Sake or pale dry
    sherry

Prepare individual servings in Japanese tea cups or small bowls. Stir together sugar, broth, soy sauce and Sake.

Deep-Fried Shrimp

Use medium to large raw fresh or frozen and defrosted shrimp. Shell shrimp, leaving tails on. Cut out the vein along the back. Butterfly very large shrimp by cutting down through the back to within ⅛ inch of other side, being careful not to split shrimp in half. Press open to flatten. Wash shrimp and pat dry.

Shrimp may be fried plain, or with Light Crumb Coating or Seasoned Breading. For a light batter, use Egg Batter or its corn meal variation, Japanese Tempura Batter or Light and Fluffy Batter. For a thicker coating, use Beer or Eggless Batter. To batter shrimp, hold them by the tails and dip into batter, allowing excess to flow back into the bowl.

Preheat oil in mini-fryer (375°). Fry shrimp, a few at a time, until golden brown, about 3 minutes. Serve with Tartar Sauce, below, Zippy Tomato Sauce, page 30, or Apricot Curry Sauce, page 34.

Tartar Sauce

⅔ cup

½ cup mayonnaise
3 tablespoons chopped cucumber
  pickle or relish
1 tablespoon capers, optional
2 teaspoons finely chopped onion
  Pinch curry powder

Combine all ingredients in a small serving bowl.

Batter Fried Shrimp or Fillets, Chinese Style

Prepare Sweet-Sour Sauce, below, in a saucepan large enough to hold sauce and fish or shrimp. Keep warm over low heat. Fry fillets or shrimp, a few at a time, and set them aside on paper towels to drain. When all are cooked, add them to the sauce and warm through. Serve with steamed rice.

Sweet-Sour Sauce

¾ cup

⅓ cup brown sugar
1 to 2 tablespoons soy sauce
⅓ cup wine vinegar
1 tablespoon cornstarch
⅓ cup water or pineapple juice
  Combination of fruits and
    vegetables from list below:
    Fresh or well-drained pineapple
      chunks
    Well-drained mandarin oranges
    Crisp-cooked green peppers
    Crisp-cooked carrots
    Crisp-cooked Chinese pea pods
    Crisp-cooked small whole onions

In a small saucepan, combine sugar, soy sauce and vinegar. Bring to a boil; cook until sugar is dissolved. Dissolve cornstarch in water or pineapple juice. Stir into sugar mixture. Cook over medium heat, stirring constantly, until mixture is thickened and clear. Add fruits and vegetables to taste. Serve with fried pork, beef, chicken or fish.

Chinese Stuffed Shrimp

2 servings

6 or 8 large, uncooked fresh or frozen, defrosted shrimp
½ cup ground or finely chopped ham*
2 water chestnuts, finely chopped
1 tablespoon snipped chives or parsley
¼ cup flour, spread on a plate or waxed paper
1 egg, slightly beaten
½ cup fine, dry bread crumbs

Shell shrimp, leaving tails on. Devein. Cut down the center back to within ⅛ to ¼-inch of other side, being careful not to split shrimp in half.

In a small bowl, mix together thoroughly, ham, water chestnuts and chives. If mixture does not hold together, add 2 tablespoons of the beaten egg and 3 tablespoons of the bread crumbs. Fill each shrimp with about 1 tablespoon stuffing. Close shrimp around filling and press openings together firmly.

Roll shrimp in flour and shake off excess. Dip in beaten egg, allowing excess egg to drain back into bowl. Roll in bread crumbs.

Preheat oil in mini-fryer (375°). Fry shrimp, a few at a time, until golden brown, 3 to 4 minutes. Drain on paper towels. Serve hot with Zippy Tomato Sauce, page 30, or Apricot Curry Sauce, page 34.

*A blender can be used to chop ham and water chestnuts.

Variation:

Anchovy Stuffed Shrimp: for the stuffing substitute a well-blended mixture of:

2 tablespoons soft butter
2 teaspoons anchovy paste
1 tablespoon finely chopped onion
2 teaspoons lime or lemon juice
⅓ cup soft bread crumbs

Substitute Beer Batter for the egg and crumb coating. Serve with Tartar Sauce, page 38, or Zippy Tomato Sauce, page 30.

Deep-Fried Fish Fillets

Use uncooked fresh or frozen, defrosted fillets. Remove any bones and cut in serving size pieces to fit fryer. If fillets are thicker than ½-inch, slice into sticks. Pat fish very dry. Frozen fillets are especially moist. Except when using Buttermilk Batter, coat them lightly with flour before breading or battering.

Other good batters are the corn meal variation of Egg Batter for a Southern flavor, Tempura, Light and Fluffy or Eggless Batter. Use either Light Crumb Coating or Seasoned Breading for breaded fillets.

Preheat oil in mini-fryer (375°). Fry pieces or sticks, a few at a time until golden brown, about 3 minutes. Serve with lemon wedges, Cucumber Sauce, page 41, or Tartar Sauce, page 38.

Shrimp Stuffed Sole

2 servings

2 to 4 fillets of fresh or frozen, defrosted sole, 5 to 7 inches long (½ to 1 pound)
Salt
Pepper
2 tablespoons lemon juice
1 tablespoon butter or margarine
1 tablespoon flour
2 tablespoons milk
1 egg, slightly beaten
Pinch curry powder
1 tablespoon Parmesan cheese
½ cup tiny or chopped cooked shrimp
1 teaspoon water
½ cup fine, dry bread crumbs, spread on a plate or waxed paper

Salt and pepper fillets. Marinate in lemon juice 30 minutes. While fish are marinating, melt butter in a small saucepan. Blend in flour. Stir in milk and half the beaten egg (about 2 tablespoons). Cook over low heat, stirring constantly, until thick. Stir in curry powder, cheese, shrimp and 1 tablespoon bread crumbs.

Dry sole fillets. Divide and spread filling on fillets. Roll up and fasten with wooden picks. Combine water with remaining egg. Roll fish in bread crumbs; dip in egg and roll in crumbs again, coating ends well.

Preheat oil in mini-fryer (375°). Fry stuffed fillets until golden brown, 4 to 5 minutes. Drain on paper towels and serve hot.

Fried Fish Balls

2 servings

2 tablespoons finely chopped onion
1 tablespoon butter or margarine
2 tablespoons flour
¼ cup milk or cream
½ teaspoon salt
Dash pepper
1 egg, slightly beaten
1 teaspoon grated lemon peel
¾ cup flaked, cooked fish or well-drained tuna or salmon
2 to 3 tablespoons flour, spread on a plate or waxed paper
1 teaspoon water
½ cup fine, dry bread crumbs, spread on a plate or waxed paper

In a small skillet or saucepan, saute onion in butter. Blend in flour. Stir in milk, salt and pepper, cook over low heat, stirring constantly, until very thick. Stir in half the beaten egg (about 2 tablespoons). Refrigerate until chilled.

Blend in lemon peel and fish. Drop by rounded tablespoons into flour, roll to coat and shape into balls. Combine remaining egg with water. Dip balls in egg mixture, allowing excess to drain back into bowl. Roll in crumbs.

Preheat oil in mini-fryer (375°). Fry balls, a few at a time, until deep golden brown, about 3 minutes. Drain on paper towels. Serve with Tartar Sauce, page 38.

Timbale Chicken Salad

Timbales

These crisp shells, filled with creamed meat or seafood, make a delicious lunch or supper main dish. Timbale shells may also be filled with buttered or creamed vegetables for a distinctive side dish. The fillings below will fill 4 shells, enough for 4 light luncheon or 2 hearty supper servings. For additional servings, the recipes can be doubled easily.

How To Make Timbales

See pages 70 and 71 for special instructions and step-by-step pictures.

Extra Timbale shells can be stored in the freezer, or extra batter may be used to make Rosettes with the addition of some sugar.

If shells become soft, crisp them in a 250° oven for about 5 minutes.

Main Dish Timbales

About 20 shells

 1 egg
¼ teaspoon salt
½ cup milk
½ cup all-purpose flour

Place timbale iron in the oil while preheating the mini-fryer (375°).

In a small mixing bowl, combine egg, salt, and half the milk. Beat on low speed until blended. Blend in the flour, then remaining milk. Beat until smooth.

Remove iron from hot oil, allowing excess to drain off. Dip the *hot* iron into batter to within ¼-inch of the top of the form. Hold the iron under hot oil until Timbale is golden brown, 1 to 1½ minutes. Remove from oil, tilting the iron so that oil drains back into the fryer. Slide Timbale off the iron.

Drain upside down on paper towels. Fill Timbale shells just before serving.

Variation:

Savory Timbales: Substitute seasoned salt (garlic, onion or celery) for salt.

49

Chicken or Turkey A La King

4 timbale shells

¼ cup chopped celery
1 can (2-oz.) mushroom pieces, drained and broth reserved
2 tablespoons chopped onion
3 tablespoons butter or margarine
3 tablespoons flour
½ cup chicken broth
½ cup light cream
1 cup cubed cooked chicken or turkey
½ cup cooked green vegetables (beans, peas, chopped broccoli), optional
¼ teaspoon salt
Dash pepper

In a heavy saucepan, saute celery, mushrooms and onion in butter. Blend in flour. Stir in mushroom broth, chicken broth and cream. Cook over medium heat, stirring constantly, until thickened. Stir in chicken, vegetables, salt and pepper and heat through. serve hot in timbale shells.

Rarebit Timbales

4 shells

2 tablespoons butter or margarine
¼ jar (2-oz.) mushroom pieces, drained
1 tablespoon flour
¾ cup milk
¾ cup shredded Cheddar or American process cheese
½ cup cubed ham, wieners or bologna
¼ teaspoon salt
Dash pepper

Melt butter in a small, heavy saucepan and saute mushrooms. Blend in flour until smooth. Stir in milk. Cook over medium heat, stirring constantly, until thickened. Stir in cheese, ham, salt and pepper and heat through. Spoon into timbale shells and serve immediately.

Creamed Peas and Eggs in Timbales

When frozen peas are added at the end and heated to serving temperature, they have the flavor and texture of fresh peas.

2 tablespoons butter or margarine
2 tablespoons flour
1 tablespoon prepared mustard
¾ cup milk
1 cup frozen peas
¼ teaspoon salt
Dash pepper
4 hard-cooked eggs, shelled

Melt butter in 1 quart saucepan. Blend in flour and mustard. Gradually stir in milk. Cook over medium heat, stirring constantly, until thickened. Stir in peas, salt and pepper, and cook until peas are heated through. Slice 1 egg into each timbale shell. Top with about ⅓ cup hot creamed peas. Serve immediately.

Variation:

Tuna Timbales: Add 1 can (6½ to 7-oz.) tuna or salmon, drained and flaked, to the cream sauce with the peas. You may substitute any cooked, chopped vegetable, such as asparagus or broccoli, for the peas. Omit eggs.

Seafood Au Gratin

4 timbale shells

1 cup (3 to 4-oz.) frozen cooked tiny shrimp, defrosted, or 1 can (4½-oz.) shrimp or other seafood, drained
½ teaspoon dill weed or seed
2 tablespoons butter or margarine
2 tablespoons flour
¾ cup milk or half and half
1 egg, slightly beaten
½ cup shredded Cheddar or American process cheese
2 teaspoons lemon juice
¼ teaspoon salt
Dash pepper

In a small bowl, combine shrimp and dill, refrigerate 1 to 2 hours. Melt butter in a small, heavy saucepan. Blend in flour. Stir in milk. Cook over medium low heat until thickened, stirring constantly. Blend some of the hot mixture into beaten egg, then stir egg mixture into sauce in pan. Cook 1 to 2 minutes, stirring constantly.

Stir in shrimp and heat through. Blend in cheese, lemon juice, salt and pepper. Just before serving, spoon hot filling into timbale shells. Garnish with toasted bread crumbs, if desired.

Variation:

Mushroom Timbales: Substitute 4 to 6-oz. fresh mushrooms, sliced, for shrimp; parsley, tarragon or chervil for dill and Swiss cheese for Cheddar. Saute mushrooms in butter before adding flour.

Timbale Chicken Salad

4 timbale shells

⅓ cup mayonnaise or salad dressing
1 tablespoon chopped green pepper
1 teaspoon finely chopped onion
¼ teaspoon salt
⅛ teaspoon curry powder
1 cup cubed cooked chicken or turkey
1 cup seedless, halved green grapes, or chopped fresh peaches
1 cup chopped or shredded lettuce

In medium bowl, combine mayonnaise, green pepper, onion, salt and curry powder. Add chicken and fruit and toss to combine well. Refrigerate until serving time. Just before serving, add lettuce, toss and pile salad into timbale shells.

Variations:

Timbale Fruit Plate: Substitute 1 cup chopped celery for fruit. Serve timbale filled with salad, surrounded with a ring of fresh fruits, such as melon, grapes, peaches, strawberries, apples, oranges, bananas.

Seafood Salad Plate: Substitute tiny cooked shrimp or crabmeat for chicken and 1 cup chopped celery for fruit. Serve timbale filled with salad surrounded by sliced tomatoes, hard-cooked eggs and cucumbers or grapefruit sections and avocado slices.

Vegetables

Almost any vegetable deep-fries well. It is a cooking method which not only gives variety to meals, but can extend the list of vegetables which you or your family like. Following is a partial list of fryable vegetables, with instructions on preparing them for cooking and suggestions for different batters. For most of these vegetables, no recipe is needed. Procedures are the same, no matter how many servings you prepare. Unless otherwise specified, frying temperature is 375°. Drain fried vegetables well on paper towels before serving.

1. *Zucchini in Seasoned Breading, page 11*
2. *Mushrooms in Buttermilk Batter, page 12*
3. *Broccoli in Japanese Tempura Batter, page 12*
4. *Carrot Fritters, page 55*

Artichoke Hearts (Frozen)

Defrost artichoke hearts thoroughly and pat them dry with paper towels. Artichoke hearts may be fried without batter. Light Crumb Coating is delicious and Egg or Beer Batter will give them a crisp crust.

Asparagus (Fresh)

Snap off and discard the tough lower ends of the asparagus. Remove the small leaves below the tips. Wash the asparagus in cold water and pat dry with paper towels. Asparagus may be fried without batter and seasoned with lemon juice or soy sauce. It is particularly good with the Light Crumb Coating, and makes a nice springtime addition to a Tempura.

Green Beans (Fresh)

Wash beans in cold water and snap off ends. Blanch beans by dropping them in boiling salted water. When the water returns to a boil, cook for 2 minutes. Drain immediately and plunge them into cold water to stop their cooking and retain fresh green color. Leave them whole or cut diagonally in 1-inch lengths. Pat dry with paper towels. Beans may be fried without batter. Italian Batter and Japanese Tempura Batter are both excellent. Try Beer Batter for a new green bean experience.

French Cut Green Beans (Fresh or Frozen)

Wash fresh beans, snap off ends and slice lengthwise. Blanch beans in boiling salted water 2 to 3 minutes. Drain and plunge into cold water. Cook frozen French cut beans as directed on package for ⅔ the recommended time. Drain and cool as above. Dry thoroughly. Place beans in a small bowl and spoon a small amount of Egg or Tempura Batter over them. Toss or turn beans with a fork, adding more batter as needed, until they are lightly coated. With metal tongs, lift out a small amount of beans, letting excess batter drain back into bowl. Fry bean fritters in hot oil until golden brown, 1 to 2 minutes. Skim oil with slotted spoon to remove bits of batter which break off.

Broccoli (Fresh)

Cut off branches where they separate from the main stalk. Halve or quarter them so the pieces are about ⅜-inch thick. With a sharp knife, strip off the skin, stopping just below flower buds. Cut off and discard the lower ½-inch of the main stalk. Halve or quarter the stalk and peel away the dark green skin to expose the tender, whitish flesh. Cut stalks into sticks ⅜-inch thick and 1½ to 2-inches long. Just before frying, wash broccoli in cold water. Drain and pat dry with paper towels. Peeled broccoli may be fried without batter, but Japanese Tempura Batter gives it a lacy crust which is attractive as well as delicious. (Frozen broccoli is not peeled and is too tough for frying.)

Carrots (Fresh)

Peel carrots. Shred lengthwise with a medium grater to make long shreds. Place shredded carrots in a small bowl. Spoon a small amount of Egg or Tempura Batter over carrots. Toss or turn carrots with a fork, adding more batter as needed, until they are lightly coated. With metal tongs, lift out a small amount of carrots, letting excess batter drain back into bowl. Fry carrot fritters in hot oil until golden brown, 1 to 2 minutes. Between batches, skim oil with slotted spoon to remove bits of batter which break off.

Cauliflower (Fresh or Frozen)

To prepare fresh cauliflower, break off flowerlets from central stalk. Wash them in cold water and cut in half. Blanch in boiling salted water for 7 to 10 minutes after water has returned to a boil. They should be tender, but still crunchy. Defrost frozen cauliflower thoroughly. (It is already blanched.) Pat cauliflowerlets dry with paper towels and use Light Crumb Coating, Seasoned Breading or Tempura Batter. Serve with a generous sprinkling of Parmesan cheese or with Cheese Sauce.

Cauliflower in Sour Cream Sauce

2 servings

12 bite-size cauliflowerlets
1 egg white
2 teaspoons milk
⅓ cup fine, dry bread crumbs spread on a plate or waxed paper
Sour Cream Sauce (below)

Clean and blanch cauliflower as directed above. In a small bowl, beat egg white and milk until blended. Dip cauliflowerlets into egg white mixture, then turn them in bread crumbs. (They may be prepared in advance and refrigerated until 15 minutes before frying time.)

Preheat oil in mini-fryer (375°). Fry 4 to 8 cauliflowerlets at a time, depending upon size of fryer, until golden brown, 1 to 2 minutes. Drain on paper towels. Pour Sour Cream Sauce over cauliflowerlets and serve immediately.

Variation:

Substitute broccoli flowers, page 54, for cauliflower. Peeled broccoli need not be blanched before frying.

Sour Cream Sauce

¼ cup dairy sour cream
1 egg yolk
2 teaspoons lemon juice
Dash pepper
Paprika

To prepare sauce, combine sour cream and egg yolk in a small saucepan. Heat almost to boiling, stirring constantly. Stir in lemon juice and pepper. Pour sauce over cauliflowerlets. Sprinkle with paprika and serve immediately.

Celery

Wash celery stems; remove leaves and scrape away any coarse strings. Cut celery in sticks ⅜-inch thick and 2 to 3 inches long. Blanch in boiling salted water 5 to 10 minutes after water has returned to a boil. Celery sticks should be tender but still crisp. Drain and pat dry with paper towels. Use Light Crumb Coating, Egg or Light and Fluffy Batter.

Corn (Frozen or Canned)

To the Basic Fritter Batter, page 45, add 1 cup frozen, whole kernel corn, defrosted and drained, or 1 can (8-oz.) whole kernel corn, well drained. Stir in 2 tablespoons chopped green pepper or pimiento. Fry as directed.

Cucumbers

Peel about ½ cucumber for 2 servings. Cut in ⅛ to ¼-inch slices. Place in bowl and cover with water. Sprinkle with salt (½ teaspoon for ½ cucumber). Let stand 30 minutes. Drain thoroughly.

Dredge cucumbers in flour; shake off excess. (Cucumbers have so much natural moisture that coatings or batters will not adhere.) Use Light Crumb Coating, Seasoned Breading, Italian, Egg or Eggless Batter. Sprinkle fried cucumbers with salt.

Eggplant

Peel the eggplant; halve or quarter it lengthwise, depending on it's size. Cut crosswise into slices ⅜-inch thick, or lengthwise into sticks ⅜-inch thick and 3 inches long. Place eggplant into a colander, salt it well and toss gently to distribute salt evenly. Set colander in a sink and allow eggplant to drain for at least 30 minutes. This removes bitterness and excess moisture. Pat dry with paper towels.

Eggplant fried in Japanese Tempura Batter has a light, crisp crust with a creamy interior. It may also be fried with Light Crumb Coating, Italian, Egg or Light and Fluffy Batter. Eggplant fried without batter absorbs more oil, but is delicious served with tomato sauce and Parmesan cheese.

Mushrooms

Wash mushrooms in cold running water; pat them dry with paper towels. Cut off a thin slice from the base of each stem. Depending on their size, halve or quarter mushrooms, or slice them ¼-inch thick. Mushrooms may be fried without batter and served with a sprinkling of garlic salt and snipped parsley. They may also be fried in Italian or Japanese Tempura Batter. Small, whole mushrooms fried in Buttermilk Batter taste much like mushroom pastries and make a delicious side dish or appetizer.

Onion Rings

Onion Rings are one of the most popular of all fried vegetables. Use large, mild-flavored onions. Peel them and slice ½-inch thick, then separate slices into rings.

All the batters are delicious with onion rings; choice depends upon personal tastes and whether you prefer to prepare them in advance or just before cooking. If you like to keep a supply of homemade onion rings in the freezer, ready for frying, use Buttermilk Batter, and dry the onions on a cake rack. When onions are dry, place cake rack in the freezer. After onions are frozen, store in plastic bags.

Green Onions (Scallions)

Wash green onions. Remove roots. Cut in 1-inch pieces, using part of the green. Pat dry with paper towels. Use Light Crumb Coating.

Parsley

Parsley is commonly used as a seasoning or garnish, but it makes a delicious vegetable when fried in Japanese Tempura Batter.

Wash parsley in cold water and shake off moisture. Remove coarse stem ends, but leave enough stem to use as a "handle". Spread parsley on paper towels to dry. A few at a time, hold parsley sprigs by the stems, dip leaves in Tempura Batter and fry just until crisp and lightly golden.

Peppers

Wash sweet green or red peppers and remove stems, seeds and fleshy ribs. Cut in strips, squares or rings. Peppers may be fried without batter, or in Italian, Japanese Tempura or Egg Batter.

Potatoes (Cooked or Canned)

This is a delicious way to dress up leftover cooked potatoes, or canned potatoes.

Small boiled new potatoes: Peel and leave whole.

Large boiled potatoes: Peel and cut in 1-inch cubes or wedges.

Baked potatoes: Peel and cut in quarters.

Small, whole canned potatoes: Drain and rinse under cold running water.

Pat dry with paper towels. All potatoes should be at room temperature. Fry plain, or use Light Crumb Coating.

Potatoes (Raw)
"French Fried" Potatoes

Use mature baking potatoes. Peel potatoes and slice as directed below. To prevent discoloring, keep cut potatoes in a bowl of cold water and cover until you are ready to fry. A handful at a time, drain potatoes thoroughly and pat dry with paper towels. Use a frying basket or slotted scoop to lower potatoes into hot oil. Fry, turning frequently, until golden brown. Drain, season with salt.

For very crisp potatoes and shorter last minute frying time, use this 2-step method. A handful at a time, fry the potatoes until all sputtering stops and they are pale gold. Drain on paper towels and let cool for at least 5 minutes. Just before serving, fry again until crisp and golden brown.

French Cut Potatoes: Slice potatoes lengthwise into strips ⅜-inch thick.

English Cut Potatoes: Slice peeled or unpeeled potatoes into lengthwise strips ½-inch thick.

Matchstick Potatoes: Slice potatoes lengthwise into strips ¼-inch thick.

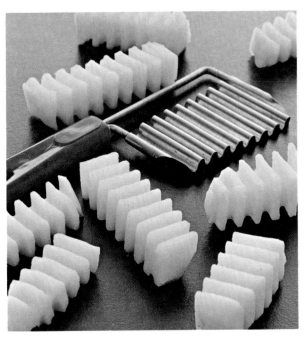

Crinkle Cut Potatoes: Using a crinkle cutter, available in housewares departments, slice potatoes lengthwise into strips ½-inch thick.

Pub Cut Potatoes: Cut peeled or unpeeled potatoes crosswise into slices ¼-inch thick.

Waffled Potatoes: Using a crinkle cutter, cut the potato crosswise into slices ¼-inch thick, giving the potato a quarter turn after each slice so that one side of each slice is crinkled horizontally and the other vertically.

Fried Potato Balls

Fried Potato Balls

2 servings (8 small balls)

These crisp balls have a good fresh potato flavor. Serve them with steak, hamburgers or chops.

1 large russet potato
¼ teapsoon salt
3 tablespoons flour
1 egg yolk*

Shred potato with medium-sized grater. (Should make ¾ to 1 cup.) Rinse shreds with cold water; drain thoroughly in a sieve, pressing out excess water. Combine salt, flour and egg yolk. Stir in potatoes.

Preheat oil in mini-fryer (375°). Drop mixture by tablespoonfuls into hot oil; fry until light golden brown, 2 to 3 minutes, turning to brown both sides, if necessary. Stir batter occasionally to keep it well combined. Drain finished potato balls on paper towels and sprinkle with salt.

*When doubling the recipe, use 1 whole egg.

Potatoes (Mashed)
Cheese Potato Puffs

2 to 4 servings (24 puffs)

Use leftover mashed potatoes, either homemade or instant, for this French specialty.

2 tablespoons butter or margarine
¼ cup water
¼ teaspoon salt
¼ cup flour
1 egg
⅔ cup mashed potatoes, warm or cold
3 tablespoons grated Parmesan cheese

In a small saucepan, stir together butter, water and salt. Bring to a full boil and reduce heat to lowest setting. Remove pan from heat and stir in flour vigorously. Return to heat; continue beating until mixture forms a ball.

Remove from heat. Add egg and beat until mixture is smooth and glossy. Blend in potatoes and cheese.

Preheat oven to lowest setting and line a baking dish with paper towels. Preheat oil in mini-fryer (350°). Drop mixture by rounded teaspoonfuls into hot oil, a few at a time. Fry until golden brown, 3 to 4 minutes. Drain on paper towels and keep warm in oven until all are fried. Serve hot.

Potato Sticks

2 servings

1 cup cold mashed potatoes*
1 egg, separated
2 tablespoons finely snipped parsley
2 tablespoons finely chopped onion
¼ teaspoon salt
    Dash pepper
⅓ cup fine, dry bread crumbs,
    spread on a plate or waxed
    paper
2 teaspoons milk

In a mixing bowl, beat together mashed potatoes, egg yolk, parsley, onion, salt and pepper until well blended. If necessary, chill for easier handling.

Drop potato mixture by rounded teaspoonfuls into bread crumbs; roll to coat. Shape into 2-inch sticks. In a small bowl, beat egg white and milk together until smooth. Dip potato sticks in egg white mixture; roll in crumbs again. (Potato sticks may be prepared in advance and refrigerated until 15 minutes before frying time.)

Preheat oil in mini-fryer (375°). Fry sticks, a few at a time, until golden brown, about 2 minutes. Drain on paper towels and serve hot.

Variation:

Omit egg white and crumb coating. Drop potato mixture by rounded teaspoonfuls into hot oil.

*To use instant potatoes, prepare 2 servings but decrease water to ½ cup.

Tomatoes (Fresh, Green)

Wash green tomatoes and slice ⅜-inch thick. Pat dry with paper towels. Fry without batter, or in Light Crumb Coating, Seasoned Breading, Italian or Beer Batter.

Tomatoes (Fresh, Ripe)

Wash ripe tomatoes and slice ¼-inch thick. Dredge slices in flour; shake off excess. (Fresh tomatoes are so moist that breadings or batters will not adhere.) Use Light Crumb Coating, Seasoned Breading, Egg or Eggless Batter.

Zucchini (Fresh)

Scrub zucchini in cold water and remove stem and tip. Cut unpeeled zucchini crosswise in ¼-inch slices or lengthwise in sticks ⅜-inch thick and 3 inches long. Pat dry with paper towels. Italian Batter is a first choice for zucchini and sticks fry more crisply than slices. Both sticks and slices are good in Japanese Tempura Batter.

Leftover Vegetable Fritters

Add 1 cup finely chopped leftover vegetables (one kind or a mixture) to Basic Fritter Batter, page 45. Fry as directed.

How To Make Rosettes

Rosettes

3½ to 4 dozen cookies

2 eggs
1 tablespoon sugar
1 teaspoon vanilla
½ teaspoon salt
1 cup milk
1 cup all-purpose flour
Confectioners' sugar

Place rosette iron in the oil while preheating the mini-fryer (375°).

Mixer method: In a small mixing bowl, combine eggs, sugar, vanilla, salt and half the milk. Beat at low speed until blended. Blend in flour, then remaining milk. Beat until smooth.

Remove iron from hot oil, allowing excess oil to drain off. Dip the *hot* iron into batter, making sure that the batter does not run over the top of the form. Hold the iron under hot oil until Rosette is golden brown, about 30 seconds. Remove from oil and slide Rosette off iron. Some Rosettes will fall off the iron while frying, and can be removed with a slotted spoon.

Drain Rosettes upside down on paper towels. Sprinkle Rosettes with confectioners' sugar, granulated sugar or a cinnamon-sugar mixture.

Blender method: Place all ingredients except confectioners' sugar in blender. Blend at medium speed 4 to 5 seconds.

Use a single iron with round mini-fryers. A double iron may be used with oblong fryers.

Iron must be hot or the batter will not stick. It may be necessary to reheat the iron between fryings.

Strain batter if it appears very lumpy, and stir it occasionally to keep it well combined while making Rosettes.

When using a double rosette iron, pour batter into a shallow casserole large enough so that both forms can be dipped at the same time.

Rosettes can be stored several weeks in an airtight container. If they become soft, crisp them in a 250° oven for about 5 minutes.

Special Tips for Timbales

Follow the instructions for making Rosettes. If a hole forms on the bottom of the shell when the hot iron is lifted out of the batter, use a spoon to fill the hole with a very thin layer of batter before placing iron in the oil for frying.

Extra Timbale shells can be stored in the freezer. They may also be sugared and served as cookies, or extra batter may be used to make Rosettes.

If shells become soft, crisp them in a 250° oven for about 5 minutes.

Mock Devonshire Cream Tarts

Dessert Timbales

about 20 shells

1 egg
2 teaspoons sugar
¼ teaspoon salt
½ teaspoon vanilla
½ cup milk
½ cup all-purpose flour

Place timbale iron in the oil while preheating the mini-fryer (375°).

In a small mixing bowl, combine egg, sugar, salt, vanilla and half the milk. Beat on low speed until blended. Blend in the flour, then remaining milk. Beat until smooth.

Remove iron from hot oil, allowing excess to drain off. Dip the *hot* iron into batter to within ¼ inch of the top of the form. Hold the iron under hot oil until Timbale is golden brown, 1 to 1½ minutes. Remove from oil, tilting the iron so that oil drains back into the fryer. Slide Timbale off the iron.

Drain upside down on paper towels. Fill Timbale shells just before serving.

Mock Devonshire Cream Tarts

12 tarts

1 package (8-oz.) cream cheese, softened
¼ cup confectioners' or granulated sugar
1 tablespoon milk
1 tablespoon grated orange or lemon peel
½ cup whipping cream
4 cups assorted fresh fruits, cut in bite-sized pieces

In a quart mixing bowl, beat cheese, sugar, milk and peel until light and fluffy. On medium speed, gradually beat in cream until mixture is smooth and thick. Refrigerate until serving time.

Just before serving, place 2 to 3 tablespoons of cream mixture in each Timbale Shell. Top with ⅓ cup of fresh fruit.

Mile High Strawberry Tarts

12 tarts

These tarts may be prepared in advance and frozen.

**1 package (10-oz.) frozen
    strawberries, partially defrosted**
½ cup sugar
1 egg white
2 teaspoons lemon juice
1 cup whipping cream

In a large mixing bowl, combine strawberries, sugar, egg white and lemon juice. Beat at high speed 5 to 8 minutes, until stiff peaks form when beaters are raised. In a chilled bowl, beat cream until stiff. Fold into strawberry mixture.

Filling may be refrigerated up to one hour, and spooned into shells just before serving. For frozen tarts, spoon the filling into the shells. Freeze tarts 2 to 4 hours until firm, then cover. If desired, decorate each tart with a fresh strawberry slice when served.

Variation:

Raspberry or Peach Tarts: Substitute frozen raspberries or peaches for the strawberries.

Ice Cream Sundae Timbales

Place a scoop of ice cream in each shell. Top with a Sundae Sauce.

Fruit Tarts

Place sliced fresh strawberries, peaches, bananas or blueberries in Timbale shells. Top with sweetened whipped cream.

Calas (Rice Fritters)

2 to 3 servings

For years, the cry of the Calas vendor, "Belle Cala, tout chaud!" was part of the picturesque tradition of New Orleans' streets.

1 egg
3 tablespoons sugar
⅓ cup all-purpose flour
1 teaspoon baking powder
¼ teaspoon salt
¼ teaspoon nutmeg
¼ teaspoon vanilla
⅔ cup cold, cooked rice*
    Confectioners' sugar
    Tart, red jelly

In a small mixing bowl, beat egg until thick and foamy. With a spoon, stir in remaining ingredients, except sugar and jelly, just until blended.

Preheat oil in mini-fryer (375°). A few at a time, drop by tablespoonfuls into hot oil. Fry until golden brown, 2 to 3 minutes. Drain on paper towels.

Sprinkle with sugar and serve hot with jelly.

*For ⅔ cup rice, prepare 1 serving instant rice as directed on package.

Carnival Knots

Oreilles de Cochon

Deep-Fried Cookies

1½ to 4 dozen

Almost every country has a version of deep-fried cookies, made from thinly-rolled dough cut or twisted into fanciful shapes. Below are a few of the possibilities. Yield depends on the shape selected.

Fattigmand (Norwegian)

3 tablespoons whipping cream
3 tablespoons sugar
3 egg yolks
½ teaspoon salt
½ teaspoon ground cardamom
½ teaspoon vanilla
1 cup all-purpose flour
   Confectioners' sugar

In a small mixing bowl, combine all ingredients except flour; beat well. Blend in flour. Divide dough in half.

On a floured surface, roll out each half to a thin rectangle 1/16-inch thick. With a pastry wheel or sharp knife, cut into 2-inch strips. Cut diagonally at 4-inch intervals to form diamonds. Make a 1-inch slit lengthwise in center of each diamond. Slip one long point of the diamond through the slit and curl it back to form a twisted diamond.

Preheat oil in mini-fryer (375°). Fry, 2 or 3 at a time, until delicately brown, 15 seconds on each side. Drain on paper towels. Sprinkle with confectioners' sugar. Store in an airtight container.

Variations:

Puffy Fattigmand (Norwegian-American): Substitute 1 whole egg for 1 of the egg yolks. Add 1½ teaspoons baking powder with cardamom. Chill before rolling. Fry 30

Fattigmand　　　　　　　　　　*Cenci*

to 60 seconds on each side until golden brown.

Csorege (Hungarian): Substitute sour cream for whipping cream. Omit cardamom.

Cenci (Italian): Substitute 1½ tablespoons rum for 1½ tablespoons whipping cream. Omit cardamom. Add 2 teaspoons grated lemon peel. Cut dough in 4×3-inch rectangles. Cut 3 lengthwise slits to within ½-inch of one end, making 4 tiny strips joined at one end. Fry strips loose for "Rags and Tatters" or twisted together for "Lovers' Knots".

Carnival Knots (Italian): Substitute white wine for cream. Omit caradmom. Cut dough in 8×½-inch strips. Tie strips in loose knots.

Milosti (Czechoslovakian): Substitute mace for cardamom. Add 2 teaspoons grated lemon peel. Cut dough into small squares and prick each square several times with a fork.

Oreilles de Cochon "Pigs Ears" (New Orleans): Substitute 1 whole egg for 1 of the egg yolks. Omit cardamom. Add 1½ teaspoons baking powder. Chill before rolling. Cut dough in 4-inch squares. Substitute Creole Glaze, below, for confectioners' sugar.

Creole Glaze

1 cup pure cane syrup or dark corn syrup
½ cup chopped pecans

In a small saucepan, combine syrup and pecans. Stir over low heat until warm and fluid. Drizzle 1 tablespoon glaze over each Pig's Ear while cookies are still warm.

75

Fried Fruit Turnovers

Fried Fruit Turnovers

9 small turnovers

**Turnover Pastry (page 42)* or
a mix**
**½ can prepared fruit pie filling
Confectioners' sugar**

Prepare pastry for a 1-crust pie. Roll out on a floured surface to a 12½-inch square. Trim edges to make a 12-inch square. Cut into 9 4-inch squares. Place 1 tablespoon fruit from pie filling on half of each square. (Remaining thickened juice may be used as topping for pudding or ice cream.) Moisten edges of pastry; fold in half to form rectangles. Seal edges well with a fork.

Preheat oil in mini-fryer (375°). Fry turnovers, a few at a time, until light golden brown, about 2 minutes on each side. Drain on paper towels. Serve slightly warm, sprinkled with confectioners' sugar.

Turnovers can be prepared in advance. Fry as many as you need, refrigerate the rest for frying next day. Let refrigerated turnovers stand at room temperature 15 minutes before frying.

Variation:

Substitute about ⅔ cup fresh berries (blueberries, raspberries or sliced strawberries) or well-drained canned apple pie slices for pie filling. Sprinkle fruit on each square with ½ teaspoon sugar and a touch of cinnamon.

*For extra-crisp Turnovers, substitute egg roll skins (6 to 7-inch), cut in quarters. Use 1 tablespoon filling. Brush well with beaten egg before sealing.

Beignets Souffles

4 to 6 servings

These French doughnuts are made with cream puff batter.

½ cup water
¼ cup butter or margarine
 1 teaspoon sugar
   Pinch salt
½ cup flour
 2 eggs
   Confectioners' sugar or Glaze
   (below)

In a small saucepan stir together water, butter, sugar and salt. Bring to a full boil and reduce heat to the lowest setting. Remove pan from heat and add all the flour at once, stirring vigorously. Return pan to heat and continue to beat until mixture leaves the sides of the pan and forms a ball.

Remove pan from heat and add eggs one at a time, beating well after each addition. Continue to beat until the dough is smooth and shiny. Set aside until ready to fry.

Preheat oil in mini-fryer (370°). Drop the dough by rounded teaspoonfuls into hot oil, a few at a time. When the underside is browned, they will turn over by themselves. When both sides are golden brown, remove them with the slotted spoon or fry basket and drain on paper towels. Sprinkle the Beignets with powdered sugar or dip them in glaze. Serve hot or at room temperature.

Beignets Souffles

Variation:

Apple Souffles: Pare and coarsely shred 1 small apple; press out excess moisture. Add with ¼ teaspoon nutmeg after beating in eggs.

Glaze

½ cup confectioners' sugar
 1 tablespoon very hot water
   Drop of food coloring

In a small bowl, beat all ingredients until smooth.

Called "Mizutaki" in Japan, Broth Fondue is delicious, fun to cook, and low in calories.

Slow Simmering

A mini-fryer with a temperature probe can also be used for slow-simmered cooking. The thermostatic control operates like the control on an electric skillet, turning the heat on periodically to maintain temperature. In the mini-fryer, you can prepare about 4 servings of the same types of foods you would prepare in a slow oven or slow cooker.

You cannot start foods in the morning and let them cook all day because most foods take 2 to 4 hours to cook. However, they do not need attention during that time. Some people like to prepare a meal the night before and have it ready to reheat the next day. Many working people use the weekend to prepare several meals for the coming week. With the mini-fryer, you can cook several dishes in one day and still have time to spare for other activities.

Most of these recipes are for 4 servings, since that amount is needed for flavor and ease in cooking. Smaller quantities require stirring and attention because of evaporation. Foods suitable for slow simmering are easy to reheat and often improve in flavor when allowed to mellow. They are also excellent for freezing in single portions.

Japanese Broth Fondue

2 servings

1 half chicken breast, skinned and boned
½ pound boneless sirloin or other tender steak
3 cups water
1 carrot, scraped and cut in ¼-inch rounds
½ pound Chinese cabbage, cut in 1-inch squares
4 to 6 small mushrooms
½ can (4-oz.) bamboo shoots, rinsed and drained
4 scallions, including part of green, cut in 1-inch lengths
3 to 4 cups chicken broth
2 servings Tempura Sauce (page 37)
Hot Mustard Dip (page 24)
Sweet-Sour Apricot Dip (page 24)

If desired, partially freeze meat for easier slicing. Slice chicken into 2×¼-inch strips, beef into strips ⅛-inch thick and 2 to 4-inches long. Bring water to a boil in fryer. Using wire basket, plunge cut carrots into boiling water. When water returns to a boil, remove and cool carrots under cold water. Drain.

To serve: Divide meat and vegetables onto 2 serving plates. Provide each person with a soup bowl, 2 fondue forks for meat and vegetables, and a table fork or chopsticks for eating. Arrange bowls of Tempura Sauce and hot steamed rice at each place; set remaining dips on table.

Measure broth into mini-fryer; set it on a mat in center of table. Bring broth to a simmer (210°).

Each person spears a piece of meat on one fork and a vegetable on the other, cooks them in broth about 1 minute and dips them in one of the 3 sauces before eating with rice. To conclude the meal, ladle some of the broth into soup bowls and serve, seasoned to taste, with remaining Tempura Sauce.

Hawaiian Chicken or Pork

2 to 4 servings

2 tablespoons butter or margarine
2 to 4 chicken fryer quarters or
    pork chops
    Salt
    Pepper
4 to 8 pineapple rings (8 or 13-oz.
    can)
¼ cup pineapple juice
1 tablespoon grated orange peel
1 tablespoon brown sugar
1 teaspoon corn starch
1 tablespoon soy sauce
    Mandarin orange segments,
      optional
    Toasted coconut

Preheat fryer to 325°. Melt butter in fryer and brown chicken or pork chops well on both sides. Reduce heat to 200°. Salt and pepper meat to taste. Top chicken or chops with pineapple rings. Add juice and orange peel. Cover and cook 2 to 2½ hours, or until meat is tender.

Carefully remove pineapple rings and meat to serving plate. Skim fat from liquid in fryer. Combine brown sugar, cornstarch and soy sauce. Stir into liquid and boil until thickened and clear. Spoon sauce over chicken; decorate with orange segments and sprinkle with toasted coconut.

Variation:

One-dish Meal, Hawaiian Style: With the pineapple rings, add ½ cup uncooked long grain rice (enough for 2 to 3 servings). Add 1¼ cups chicken broth with the pineapple juice and peel. Omit brown sugar, cornstarch and soy sauce thickening.

Doubling Up (Pepper Beef and Beef Stroganoff)

Prepare 2 meals in the time it takes to cook one.

2 pounds round steak
2 tablespoons butter or margarine
1 large onion, sliced
½ cup water
1 teaspoon salt
⅛ teaspoon pepper
½ clove garlic, finely chopped

Cut beef into thin strips. (For easier slicing, partially freeze meat.) Melt butter in fryer and brown beef (325°). Reduce heat to 200°. Add remaining ingredients. Cover and cook 3½ to 4 hours, or until meat is tender. Remove half the mixture to a storage container. Cool and refrigerate for use the following day, or freeze for future use.

Pepper Beef

To remaining meat mixture in fryer, add half a green pepper, cut in ¼-inch strips. Cover and cook 200° 5 minutes. In a small saucepan, melt 1 tablespoon butter; blend in 1 tablespoon flour. Add to meat and cook until thickened. Serve hot over cooked rice.

Beef Stroganoff

Drain beef, reserving ½ cup broth. Prepare Stroganoff Sauce, page 33, substituting broth for water. Add beef strips before sour cream. Bring to a boil. Stir in sour cream, salt and pepper and heat through. Serve hot over cooked noodles.

Split Pea Soup

4 or 5 servings

1 small ham bone with some meat left on, or 1 ham hock
1 cup (8-oz.) dried split peas
½ cup chopped onion
1 carrot, diced
1 branch celery, diced
4 cups water
½ teaspoon salt
⅛ teaspoon pepper

Combine all ingredients in mini-fryer. Cover; cook at 200° 3 to 4 hours.* Remove ham bone; cut off meat and return meat to soup. If soup is too thick, thin with another cup of water and reheat.

*Ham hock will take longer to cook than ham bone.

Chow Mein Casserole

4 servings

1 pound chow mein meat or lean ground beef
½ cup chopped onion
1 teaspoon salt
⅛ teaspoon pepper
1 can (10¾-oz.) cream of mushroom soup
1½ can water
1½ cups chopped celery
¾ cup long grained rice, uncooked
2 tablespoons soy sauce

Preheat mini-fryer to 325°. Brown meat and onion, adding about 1 tablespoon salad oil or shortening, if necessary. Reduce heat to 200°. Stir in remaining ingredients. Cover, cook 2 hours.

Homemade Chili

4 to 6 servings

Chili tastes even better the second day.
It freezes well, too.

1 pound ground beef
1 medium onion, sliced
¼ cup chopped green pepper
1 can (16-oz.) tomatoes, undrained
1 can (15-oz.) kidney beans,
**   undrained**
1 bay leaf
1 to 2 teaspoons chili powder
1 teaspoon salt

Preheat mini-fryer to 325°. Brown beef;
drain off fat. Reduce heat to 200°. Stir
in remaining ingredients. Cover and
cook 3 to 4 hours. Thin chili with a
small amount of water, if desired.

Swiss Steak

2 to 4 servings

3 tablespoons flour
1 teaspoon salt
2 twists freshly ground pepper
1½ to 2 pounds Swiss or round steak
2 tablespoons salad oil or
**   shortening**
1 can (8-oz.) tomatoes, undrained
½ cup water
½ cup chopped onion
¼ cup green pepper

Combine flour, salt and pepper. Pound
into both sides of meat, using a meat
mallet or the edge of a saucer. Cut meat
into serving size pieces. Preheat mini-
fryer to 325°. Add oil and brown meat
on both sides. Reduce heat to 200°. Stir
in remaining ingredients. Cover; cook

2½ to 3 hours, or until meat is tender.
Serve with rice, noodles or potatoes.

Variation:

Creamy Swiss Steak: Substitute 1 can
(10¾-oz.) cream of mushroom soup for
tomatoes.

Four Bean Picnic Hot Dish

4 to 6 servings

Try this as a change from baked beans.

4 types of beans listed below:
**   1 can (8 to 10-oz.) Pork and**
**   Beans or Baked Beans**
**   2 to 3 cans (8 to 10-oz.) Lima,**
**   Butter, Green, or Wax Beans**
**   1 to 2 cans (15 to 16-oz.) Pinto,**
**   Kindey or Garbanzo Beans**
4 wieners or precooked sausages,
**   sliced diagonally in ½-inch pieces**
¼ cup chopped onion
¼ cup catsup or chili sauce
¼ cup brown sugar or molasses
1 tablespoon prepared mustard
**   Dash Worcestershire sauce**

Drain beans packed in clear liquid.
Use liquid from pork and beans and/or
baked beans. Combine all ingredients
in mini-fryer. Cover; cook at 200° for
2½ hours. Serve hot.

Variation:

Substitute 1 cup cubed ham, ¼ pound
chopped bacon or ½ pound ground beef
for wieners. Fry bacon or ground beef
in mini-fryer set at 325°, and drain off
fat before adding remaining ingredients.

Company Wild Rice

4 servings

¼ cup butter or margarine
½ cup thinly sliced celery, cut
    diagonally
⅓ cup chopped onion
1 can (4-oz.) mushroom pieces,
    undrained
2 cups water
1 tablespoon instant chicken bouillon
    granules
½ teaspoon salt
½ cup uncooked wild rice
¼ cup uncooked barley

Preheat mini-fryer to 325°. Melt butter
and saute onion and celery. Reduce
heat to 200°. Stir in remaining
ingredients. Cover; cook 2 hours or
until liquid is absorbed.

Variation:

One-dish Wild Rice Casserole: Brown
chicken fryer pieces or pork chops in
fryer before browning celery and onion.
Cook with rice and barley, as above.

Easy Beef Stew

4 servings

*Potatoes and carrots may be added at
the beginning or after 2 hours of
cooking.*

¼ cup butter or margarine
1 to 1½ pounds beef stew meat
1 large onion, thinly sliced
3½ cups water
1½ teaspoon salt
2 twists freshly ground pepper
1 bay leaf
2 potatoes, peeled and quartered
3 carrots, peeled and cut in thirds

Preheat mini-fryer to 325°. Melt butter
in fryer and brown meat and onions

about 10 minutes, stirring occasionally.

Reduce heat to 200°. Stir in remaining
ingredients. Cover and cook without
stirring about 3 hours, or until meat is
tender.

Remove meat and vegetables to serving
bowl. If thicker gravy is desired, melt 2
tablespoons butter or margarine in a
small saucepan; blend in 2 tablespoons
flour. Stir mixture into gravy and boil
about 2 minutes. Pour over meat and
vegetables. Serve hot.

Barbecued Spareribs

2 servings

2 pounds spareribs or country style
    ribs
⅓ cup chili sauce or catsup
3 tablespoons brown sugar
2 tablespoons soy sauce
1 teaspoon monosodium glutamate,
    optional
½ teaspoon salt
½ teaspoon smoke sauce
1 tablespoon cornstarch dissolved in
    1 tablespoon water, optional

Cut ribs into serving pieces to fit fryer.
In a 1 cup measure, combine
remaining ingredients and pour over
ribs in fryer. Let stand about 1 hour,
turning ribs over once or twice. Set
thermostat to 200°. Cover and cook
3½ hours, or until tender.* Remove
ribs and brown over hot charcoal or
under oven broiler, 10 to 15 minutes,
watching carefully. If sauce is desired,
skim fat from juices in fryer. Add
cornstarch mixture and boil until clear.
Spoon sauce over ribs.

*Country style ribs may take less
cooking time.

Consumer Guide

Mini-fryers are America's most popular new small appliance. Additional makes and models appear regularly. On the following pages you will find descriptions of the materials, capacity, features and accessories for the fryers which were available for testing at the time of publication.

Since the amount of food which can be cooked at one time depends upon the frying surface as well as oil capacity, we have measured all fryers at the recommended oil level. All of the fryers provide adequate depth to contain bubbling. Since they differ, we have provided this measurement as well. You may prefer greater depth as an added safety precaution, or shallower depth for ease in frying.

Most mini-fryers are designed to heat to the average frying temperature of 375° during the recommended preheat time, making a deep-fat thermometer unnecessary. However, before using your fryer the first time, you may want to check it with a thermometer. Since fryers of the same make and model can differ, your fryer may take less or more time to preheat.

If a deep-fat thermometer is not available, you may test the oil temperature, using 1-inch square cubes of bread. Preheat the oil in the fryer as directed by the manufacturer. Drop in a cube of bread and time it for sixty seconds. If the bread is golden brown, the temperature is approximately 375°. If the cube is under or over-done, allow the oil to cool to room temperature and repeat the test, adjusting the preheat time accordingly.

Mini-fryers With Heat Control

The heating element in most mini-fryers goes on when the fryer is plugged into an electrical outlet, and continues to heat until the appliance is unplugged. Mini-fryers with built-in thermostats turn on and off to maintain a temperature which is either pre-set by the manufacturer or regulated by the user in the same way as an electric skillet.

In either case, an on-off light indicates when the fryer is heating and when it is ready to use. Instead of preheating a specified time, you simply wait for the light to go off. If you are frying several batches of food, the fryer will signal when the oil has recovered temperature and will turn off to prevent overheating and smoking if you are interrupted by a phone call and can't add new food.

Mini-fryers with a variable heat control, similar to an electric skillet, can be used for other types of cooking, such as Cheese or Dessert Fondue and Slow Simmering. See the Slow Simmering recipe section, beginning on page 79.

Cream Cheese
  Ham Turnover Filling, and, 22
  Tuna Turnover Filling, 22
Creamy Swiss Steak, 82
Creole Glaze, 75
Crinkle Cut Potatoes, 58
Crisp-Fried Tortilla Wedges, 20
Croquettes
  Basic, 47
  Fillings for, 47
    Beef, Pork, Lamb or Veal, 47
    Chicken, 47
    Chicken and Oyster, 47
    Egg, 47
    Ham, 47
    Ham and Cheese, 47
    Rice, 47
    Salmon, 47
    Seafood, 47
    Tuna, 47
    Turkey, 47
Croutons, 14
Csorege (Hungarian), 75
Cucumbers, 56
Cucumber Sauce, 41
Curry or Mustard Dip, 30

D
Deep-Fried Beef or Pork
  Stroganoff, 33
Deep-Fried Cookies
  Carnival Knots (Italian), 75
  Cenci (Italian), 75
  Csorege (Hungarian), 75
  Fattigmand (Norwegian), 74
  Milosti (Czechoslovakian), 75
  Oreilles de Cochon ''Pig's Ears''
    (New Orleans), 75
  Puffy Fattigmand (Norwegian-
    American), 74
Deep-Fried Chicken Fryer Pieces,
  Precooked, 34
Deep-Fried Chicken, Uncooked, 35
Deep-Fried Fish Fillets, 39
Deep-Fried Shrimp, 38
Desserts
  Apple Souffles, 77
  Beignets Souffles, 77
  Calas (Rice Fritters), 73
  Carnival Knots (Italian), 75
  Cenci (italian), 75
  Csorege (Hungarian), 75
  Fattigmand (Norwegian), 74
  Fried Fruit Turnovers, 76
  Fruit Fritters, 69
  Fruit Tarts, 73
  Fruit Tempura, 69
  Ice Cream Sundae Timbales, 73

Mile High Strawberry Tarts, 73
Milosti (Czechoslovakian), 75
Mock Devonshire Cream
  Tarts, 72
Oreilles de Cochon ''Pigs' Ears''
  (New Orleans), 75
Peach Tarts, 73
Puffy Fattigmand, (Norwegian-
  American), 74
Raspberry Tarts, 73
Rosettes, 71
Timbales, 72
Dips
  Chili Con Queso, 20
  Curry or Mustard, 30
  Hot Mustard, 24
  Sour Cream-Scallion, 20
  Sweet-Sour Apricot, 24
Doubling Up (Pepper Beef and
  Beef Stroganoff), 81
Doughnuts, 63
  Applesauce Drop, 65
  Apple Souffles, 77
  Banana Balls, 65
  Beignets Souffles, 77
  Buttermilk, 65
  Cake, 64
  Flavored Sugar, 66
  Honey-Nut Balls, 65
  How to Make, 64
  Icings, 67
  Orange Drops, 66
  Orange-Nut, 65
  Sour Cream, 65

E
Easy Beef Stew, 83
Easy Chicken Egg Roll Filling, 24
Eggs
  Batter, 12
  Buttermilk Batter, 12
  Creamed Peas in
    Timbales, and, 50
  Croquette Filling, 47
  Japanese Tempura Batter, 12
  Light and Fluffy Batter, 13
  Main Dish Timbales, 49
  Pastie Filling, 43
  Rolls, 23
  Seasoned Breading, 11
Eggplant, 56
English Cut Potatoes, 58

F
Fattigmand, 74
Fillings
  Chinese Egg Roll, 23
  Cocktail Nuggets, for, 26
    Bacon-Olive, 26
    Cheese-Olive, 26
    Mexican Beef, 27
    Oriental Shrimp, 27
    Reuben, 27
    Tuna-Olive, 26
  Croquettes, for, 47
    Beef, Pork, Lamb or Veal, 47
    Chicken, 47
    Chicken and Oyster, 47
    Egg, 47
    Ham, 47
    Ham and Cheese, 47
    Rice, 47
    Salmon, 47
    Seafood, 47
    Tuna, 47
    Turkey, 47
  Easy Chicken Egg Roll, 24
  Ham and Cheese, 24
  Pasties, for, 42
    Beef, 43
    Chicken, 43
    Egg, 43
    Ham, 43
    Tuna, 43
  Pizza, 24
  Savory Turnover, for, 22
    Beef and Pickle, 22
    Chili Beef 'n' Cheese, 22
    Ham and Cream Cheese, 22
    Ham or Sausage and Cheese, 22
    Hot Dog, 22
    Onion-Pepper, 22
    Shrimp and Sour Cream, 22
    Tuna Cream Cheese, 22
    Wieners in Blankets, 22
Fish
  Batter Fried, Chinese Style, 38
  Deep-Fried Fillets, 39
  Fried Balls, 40
  Fritters, 45
  Shrimp Stuffed Sole, 40
  Tempura, 37
Flavored Sugar for Doughnuts, 66
Fondue
  Bourguignonne, 30
  Corn Dog, 32
  Frank, 32
  Hawaiian Meatballs, 32
  Japanese, 31
  Japanese Broth, 79
  Meatball Fondue, 32
  Meatball Stroganoff, 32
  Roman Meatballs, 32

Four Bean Picnic Hot Dish, 82
Frank Fondue, 32
French Cut Green Beans, fresh or frozen, 54
French Cut Potatoes, 58
French Fried Almonds, 18
French Fried Potatoes, 58
French Toastwiches, 25
Fried Cheese, 18
Fried Fish Balls, 40
Fried Fruit Turnovers, 76
Fried Pasties, 42
Fried Potato Balls, 60
Fritters
  Bacon, 45
  Calas (Rice Fritters), 73
  Chicken, Beef or Pork, 45
  Fish, 45
  Ham, 45
  Ham 'n' Pineapple or Corn, 45
  Leftover Vegetable, 61
  Oyster or Clam, 45
  Seafood, 45
  Shrimp or Crab, 45
  Tuna or Salmon, 45
Fruit Fritters, 69
Fruit Tarts, 73
Fruit Tempura, 69

G

Garnishments
  Breadings, Seasoned, 11
  Croutons, 14
  Nuts, 14
Glaze, 77
Green Beans, fresh, 54
Green Onions (Scallions), 57
Green Pepper, 57
Ground Beef
  Chili Beef 'n' Cheese Turnover Filling, 22
  Chili, Homemade, 82
  Chow Mein Casserole, 81
  Mexican Beef Cocktail Nugget Filling, 27
  Pastie Filling, 43
  Pizza Filling, 24
  Tostada Filling, 21

H

Ham
  Cheese Croquette Filling, and, 47
  Cheese Eggroll Filling, and, 24
  Chinese Stuffed Shrimp, 39
  Cream Cheese, Turnover Filling, and, 22
  Croquette Filling, 47
  Fritters, 45
  'n' Pineapple or Corn Fritters, 45
  Pastie Filling, 43
  Rarebit Timbales, 50
  Reuben Filling, 27
  Sausage and Cheese Turnover Filling, or, 22
  Split Pea Soup, 81
Hamburger
  Chili Beef 'n' Cheese Turnover Filling, 22
  Chili, Homemade, 82
  Chow Mein Casserole, 81
  Mexican Beef Cocktail Nugget Filling, 27
  Pastie Filling, 43
  Pizza Filling, 24
  Tostada Filling, 21
Hawaiian Chicken or Pork, 80
Hawaiian Meatballs, 32
Hollandaise Sauce, 30
Homemade Chili, 82
Honey-Nut Drop Doughnut Balls, 65
Honey-Nut Glaze, 65
Hot Dog Turnover Filling, 22
Hot Fried Olives, 18
Hot Mustard Dip, 24
Hot Snacks
  French Fried Almonds, 18
  Italian Rice-Cheese Balls, 48
  Popcorn, 19
  Tostada Chips, 21
Hush Puppies, 63

I

Ice Cream Sundae Timbales, 73
Icings
  Browned Butter, 67
  Chocolate, 67
  Orange, 66
  Vanilla, 67
Italian Batter, 11
Italian Rice-Cheese Balls, 48

J

Japanese Broth Fondue, 79
Japanese Tempura Batter, 12
Japanese Fondue, 31

L

Lamb Croquette Filling, 47
Leftover Vegetable Fritters, 61
Light and Fluffy Batter, 13
Light Crumb Coating, 11

M

Main Dishes, 29
  Anchovy Stuffed Shrimp, 39
  Batter Fried Shrimp or Fillets, Chinese Style, 38
  Chicken Kiev, 35
  Chicken or Turkey A La King, 50
  Chinese Stuffed Shrimp, 39
  Chow Mein Casserole, 81
  Corn Dog Fondue, 32
  Creamed Peas and Eggs in Timbales, 50
  Deep-Fried Beef or Pork Stroganoff, 33
  Deep-Fried Chicken Fryer Pieces, Precooked, 34
  Deep-Fried Chicken, Uncooked, 35
  Deep-Fried Fish Fillets, 39
  Deep-Fried Shrimp, 38
  Doubling Up (Pepper Beef and Beef Stroganoff), 81
  Easy Beef Stew, 83
  Fondue Bourguignonne, 30
  Frank Fondue, 32
  Fried Fish Balls, 40
  Hawaiian Chicken or Pork, 80
  Italian Rice-Cheese Balls, 48
  Japanese Broth Fondue, 79
  Japanese Fondue, 31
  Mushroom Timbales, 51
  One-Dish Meal, Hawaiian Style, 80
  One-Dish Wild Rice Casserole, 83
  Pasties, 42
  Rarebit Timbales, 50

Salmon Timbales, 50
Seafood Au Gratin, 51
Seafood Salad Plate, 51
Shrimp Stuffed Sole, 40
Sweet-Sour Deep-Fried Pork
  or Beef, 33
Tempura, 37
Timbale Chicken Salad, 51
Timbale Fruit Plate, 51
Timbales, 49
Tuna Timbales, 50
Marinade for Uncooked
  Chicken, 35
Matchstick Potatoes, 58
Meatball Fondue, 32
Meatball Stroganoff, 32
Mexican Beef Filling, 27
Mile High Strawberry Tarts, 73
Milosti (Czechoslovakian), 75
Mini Bismarks, 66
Mini Long Johns, 66
Mock Devonshire Cream Tarts, 72
Mushrooms, 56
  Stroganoff Sauce, 33
  Timbales, 51

N

Nacho Filling, 21
Noodles, Chinese Fried, 15
Nutmeg Icing, 67
Nuts, 14
  Almonds, French Fried, 18
  Honey Drop Doughnut Balls, 65
  Honey Glaze, 65
  Orange Doughnuts, 65

O

Olives
  Bacon Cocktail Nugget
    Filling, 27
  Cheese Cocktail Nugget
    Filling, 26
  Hot Fried, 18
  Tuna Filling, 26
One-Dish Meal, Hawaiian
  Style, 80
One-Dish Wild Rice Casserole, 83
Onion
  Green (Scallions), 57
  Pepper Turnover Filling, 22
  Rings, 15, 57
  Sour Cream Dip, 20

Orange Doughnut Drops, 66
Orange Icing, 66
Orange-Nut Doughnuts, 65
Oreilles de Cochon "Pigs' Ears"
  (New Orleans), 75
Oriental Shrimp Filling, 27
Oysters
  Chicken Croquette
    Filling, and, 47
  Fritters, 45
  Seafood Cheese Puffs, 25

P

Parmesan Cheese Puffs
  (Profiteroles), 25
Parsley, 57
Pasties
  Fillings for, 43
  Beef, 43
  Chicken, 43
  Egg, 43
  Ham, 43
  Tuna, 43
  Fried, 42
Peach Tarts, 73
Pepper Beef, 81
Peppers, 57
Pizza Filling, 24
Popcorn, 18
Pork
  Chinese Egg Roll Filling, 23
  Croquette Filling, 47
  Deep-Fried Stroganoff, 33
  Fritters, 45
  Hawaiian, 80
  One-Dish Meal, Hawaiian
    Style, 80
  Sweet-Sour Deep-Fried, 33
Potatoes
  Cooked or Canned, 57
  Crinkle Cut, 58
  English Cut, 58
  French Cut, 58
  French Fried, 58
  Fried Balls, 60
  Mashed, Cheese Potato Puffs, 60
  Matchstick, 58
  Pub-Cut, 58
  Raw, 58
  Sticks, 61
  Waffled, 58
Puffy Fattigmand (Norwegian-
  American), 74

R

Rarebit Timbales, 50
Raspberry Tarts, 73
Reuben Filling, 27
Reuben Rolls, 24
Rice Croquette Filling, 47
Riviera Cheese Puffs, 25
Roman Meatballs, 32
Rosettes, 71

S

Salmon
  Croquette Filling, 47
  Fried Fish Balls, 40
  Fritters, 45
  Timbales, 50
Sandwiches
  French Toastwiches, 25
Sauces
  Apricot Curry, 34
  Cucumber, 41
  Hollandaise, 30
  Sour Cream, 55
  Sour Cream Horseradish, 30
  Stroganoff, 33
  Sweet-Sour, 38
  Tartar, 38
  Tempura, 37
  Zippy Tomato, 30
Sausage or Ham and Cheese
  Turnover Filling, 22
Savory Fried Turnovers, 22
Savory Timbales, 49
Savory Turnover Fillings, 22
Seafood Au Gratin, 51
Seafood Cheese Puffs, 25
Seafood Croquette Filling, 47
Seafood Fritters, 45
Seafood Salad Plate, 51
Seasoned Breading, 11
Short-Cut Fruit Rolls, 64
Shrimp
  Anchovy Stuffed, 39
  Batter Fried, Chinese Style, 38
  Chinese Egg Roll Filling, 23
  Chinese Stuffed, 39
  Deep-Fried, 38
  Fritters, 45
  Oriental Filling, 27
  Seafood Au Gratin, 51
  Seafood Cheese Puffs, 25
  Seafood Croquette Filling, 47
  Sour Cream Turnover
    Filling, and, 22

Stuffed Sole, 40
Tempura, 37
Sopapillas (Mexican Fried
  Bread), 63
Sour Cream
  Doughnuts, 65
  Horseradish Sauce, 30
  Sauce, 55
  Scallion Dip, 20
  Shrimp Turnover Filling, and, 22
  Stroganoff Sauce, 33
Split Pea Soup, 81
Stroganoff Sauce, 33
Sweet-Sour Apricot Dip, 24
Sweet-Sour Deep-Fried Pork
  or Beef, 33
Sweet-Sour Sauce, 38
Swiss Steak, 82

T

Tartar Sauce, 38
Tarts
  Fruit, 73
  Mile High Strawberry, 73
  Mock Devonshire Cream, 72
  Peach, 73
  Raspberry, 73
Tempura, 37
Tempura Sauce, 37
Timbales
  Chicken or Turkey A La King, 50
  Chicken Salad, 51
  Creamed Peas and Eggs in, 50
  Dessert, 72
  Fruit Plate, 51
  How to Make, 49
  Ice Cream Sundae, 73
  Main Dish, 49
  Mushroom, 51
  Rarebit, 50
  Salmon, 50
  Seafood Au Gratin, 51
  Seafood Salad Plate, 51
  Special Tips, 71
  Tuna, 50
Tomato
  Fresh, Green, 61
  Fresh, Ripe, 61
  Zippy Sauce, 30
Tostada Chips, 21
Tostada Filling, 21

Tuna
  Cream Cheese Turnover
    Filling, 22
  Croquette Filling, 47
  Fried Fish Balls, 40
  Fritters, 45
  Olive Cocktail Nugget Filling, 26
  Pastie Filling, 43
  Timbales, 50
Turkey A La King, 50
Turkey Croquette Filling, 47
Turnovers
  Fried Fruit, 76
  Pastry, 42
  Savory Fillings, 22
  Savory Fried, 22

V

Vanilla Icing, 67
Veal Croquette Filling, 47
Vegetables, 53
  Artichoke Hearts, frozen, 54
  Asparagus, fresh, 54
  Broccoli, fresh, 54
  Carrots, fresh, 55
  Cauliflower, fresh or frozen, 55
  Cauliflower in Sour Cream
    Sauce, 55
  Celery, 56
  Corn, frozen or canned, 56
  Cucumbers, 56
  Eggplant, 56
  French Cut Green Beans, fresh
    or frozen, 54
  Green Beans, fresh, 54
  Leftover Fritters, 61
  Mushrooms, 56
  Mushroom Timbales, 51
  Onion Rings, 57
  Parsley, 15, 57
  Peppers, 57
  Potatoes
    Canned, 57
    Cooked, 57
    Crinkle Cut, 58
    English Cut, 58
    French Cut, 58
    French Fried, 58
    Fried Balls, 60

    Mashed Cheese Potato Puffs, 60
    Matchstick, 58
    Pub-Cut, 58
    Raw, 58
    Sticks, 61
    Waffled, 58
  Tomatoes, Green & Ripe, 61
  Zucchini, fresh, 61

W

Waffled Potatoes, 58
Wieners
  Corn Dog Fondue, 32
  Four Bean Picnic Hot Dish, 82
  Frank Fondue, 32
  Hot Dog Turnover Filling, 22
  In Blankets, 22
  Rarebit Timbales, 50

Z

Zippy Tomato Sauce, 30
Zucchini, fresh, 61

Credits: Cy DeCosse and Associates, especially Michael Jensen, photographer and Margaret McInerny, production coordinator
Special thanks to: Sylvia Ogren, home economist